The photo journal

man man

Peter Slater

Printed in the United States of America

"Man is the only creature who refuses to be what he is." ...

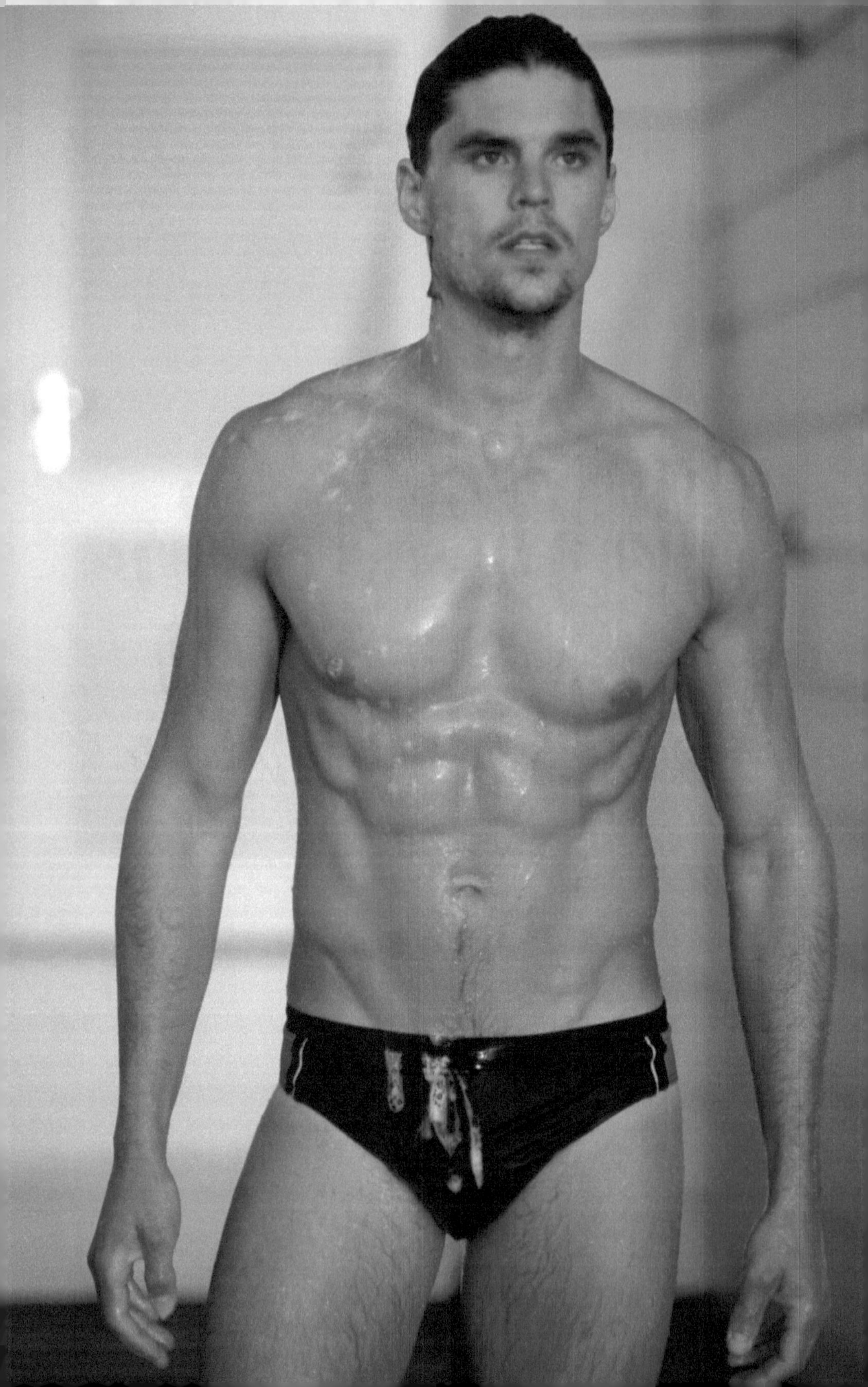

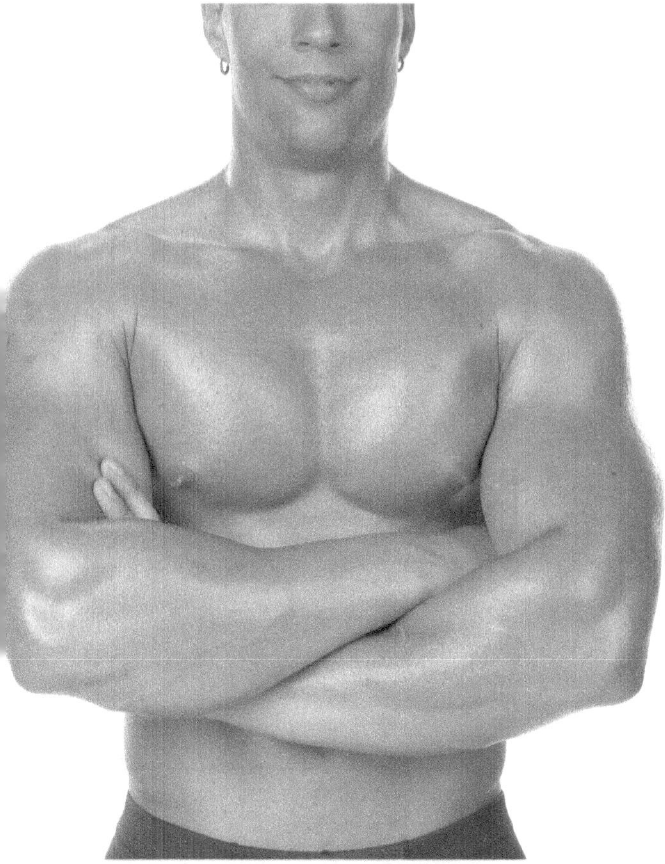
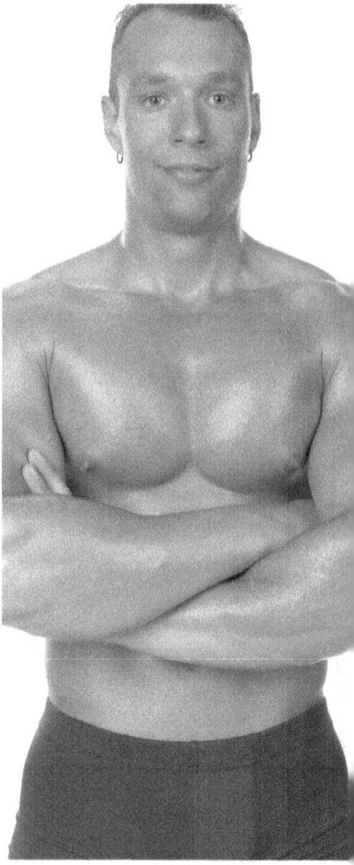
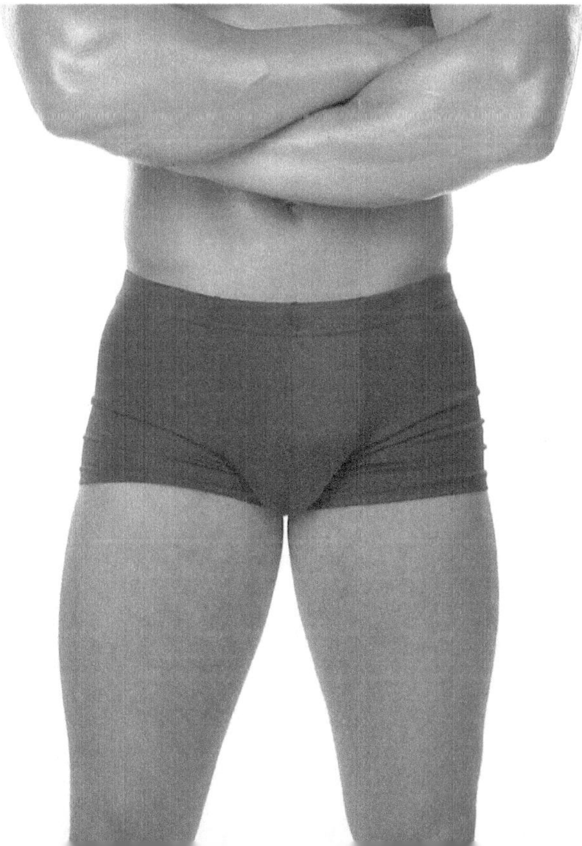
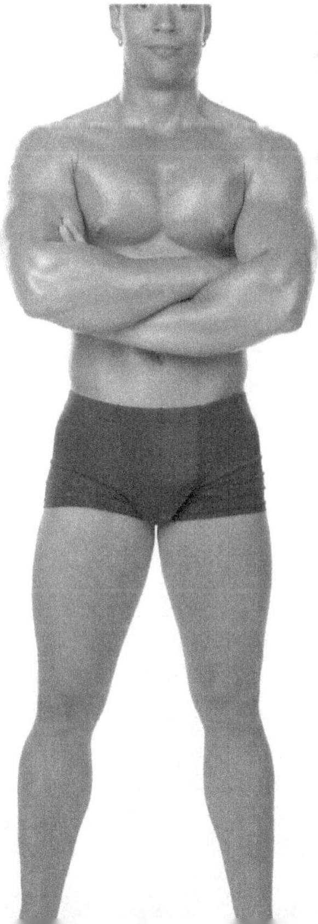

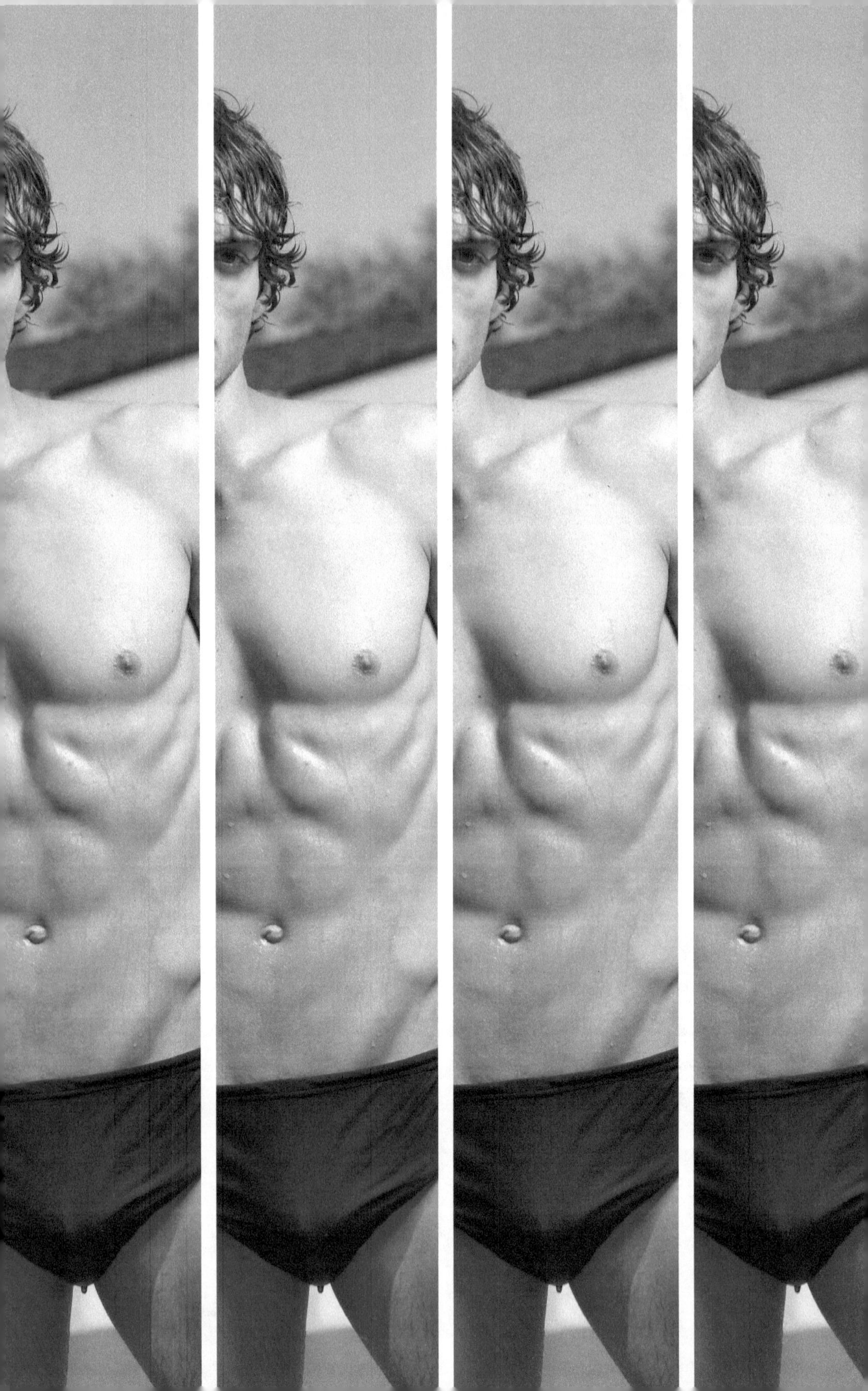

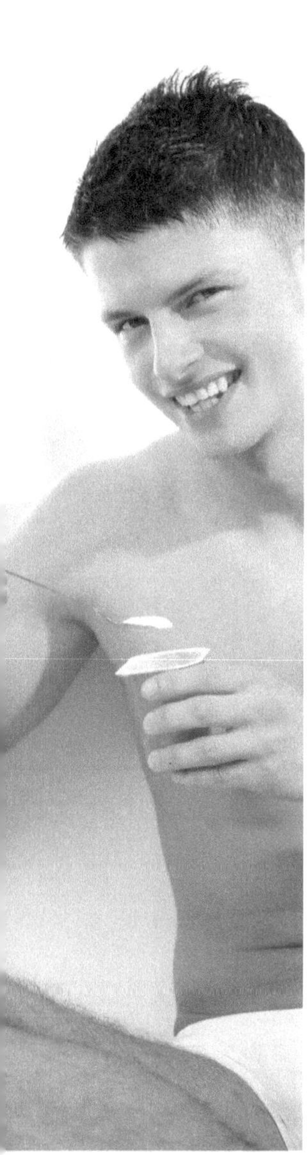

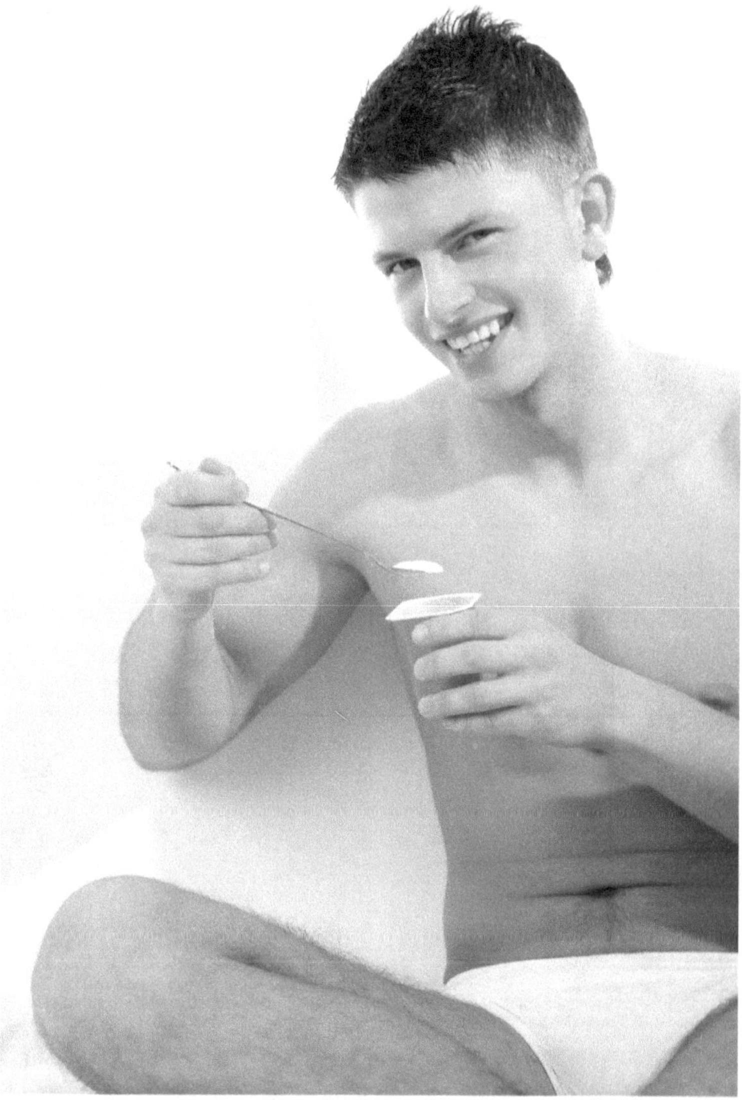

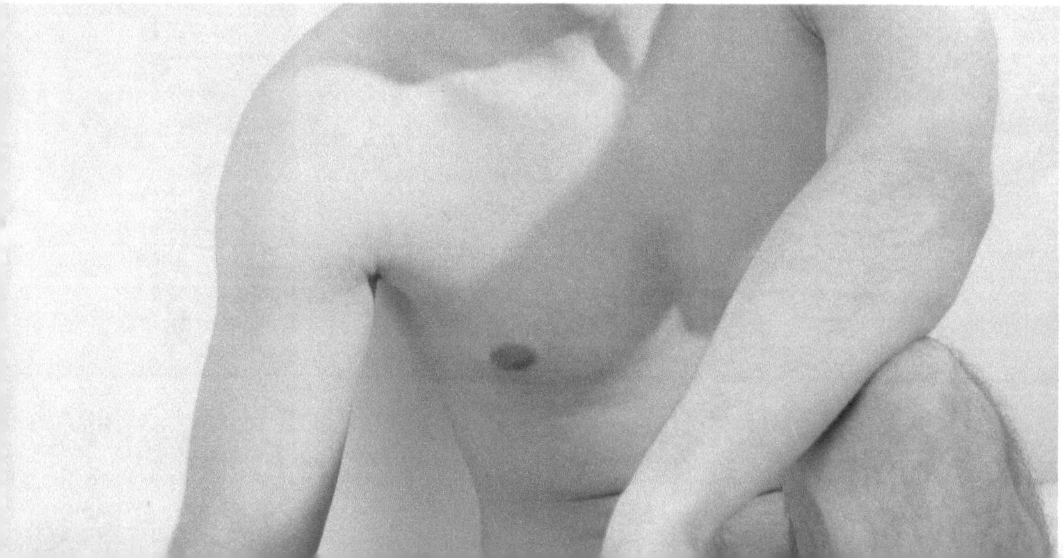

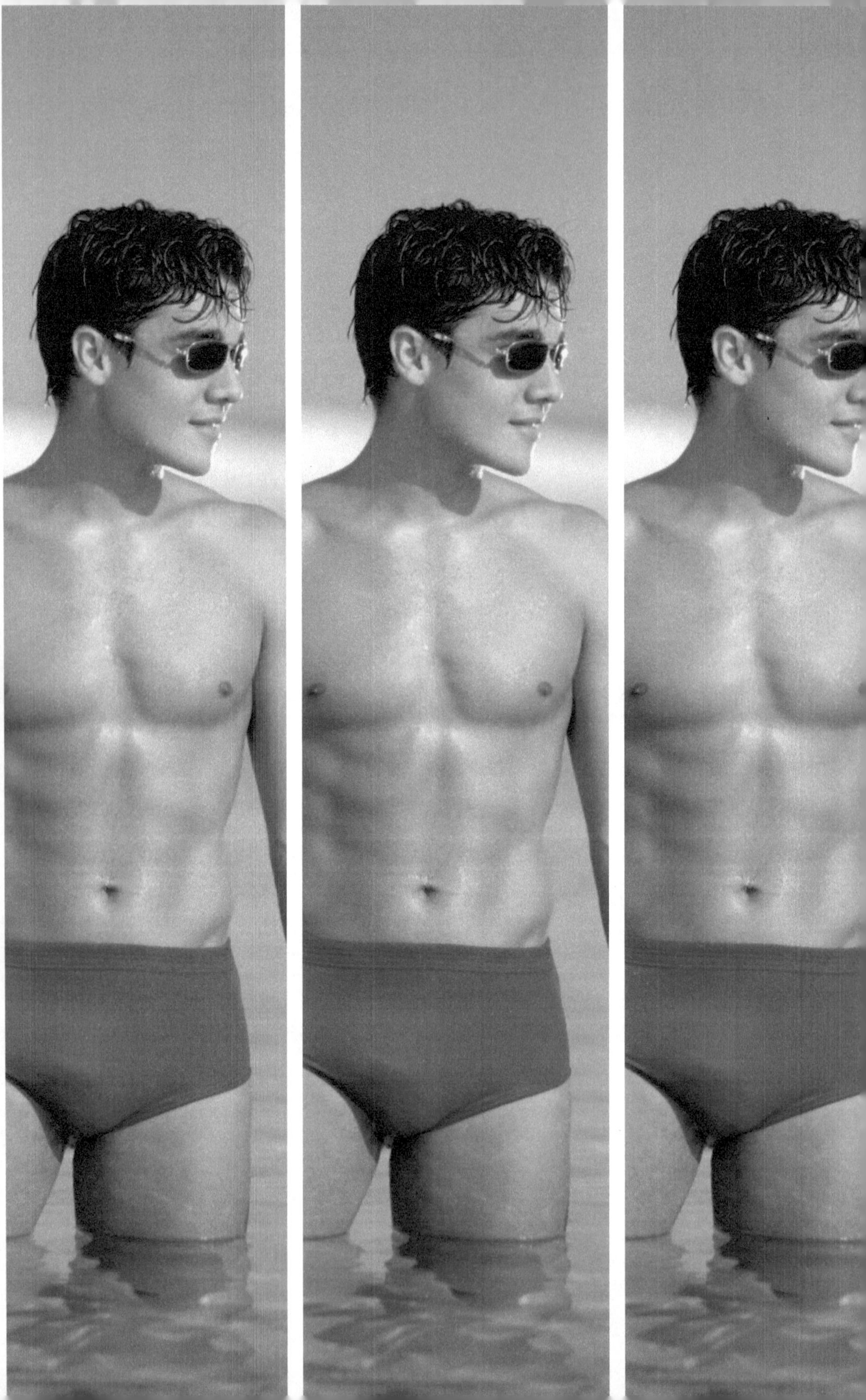

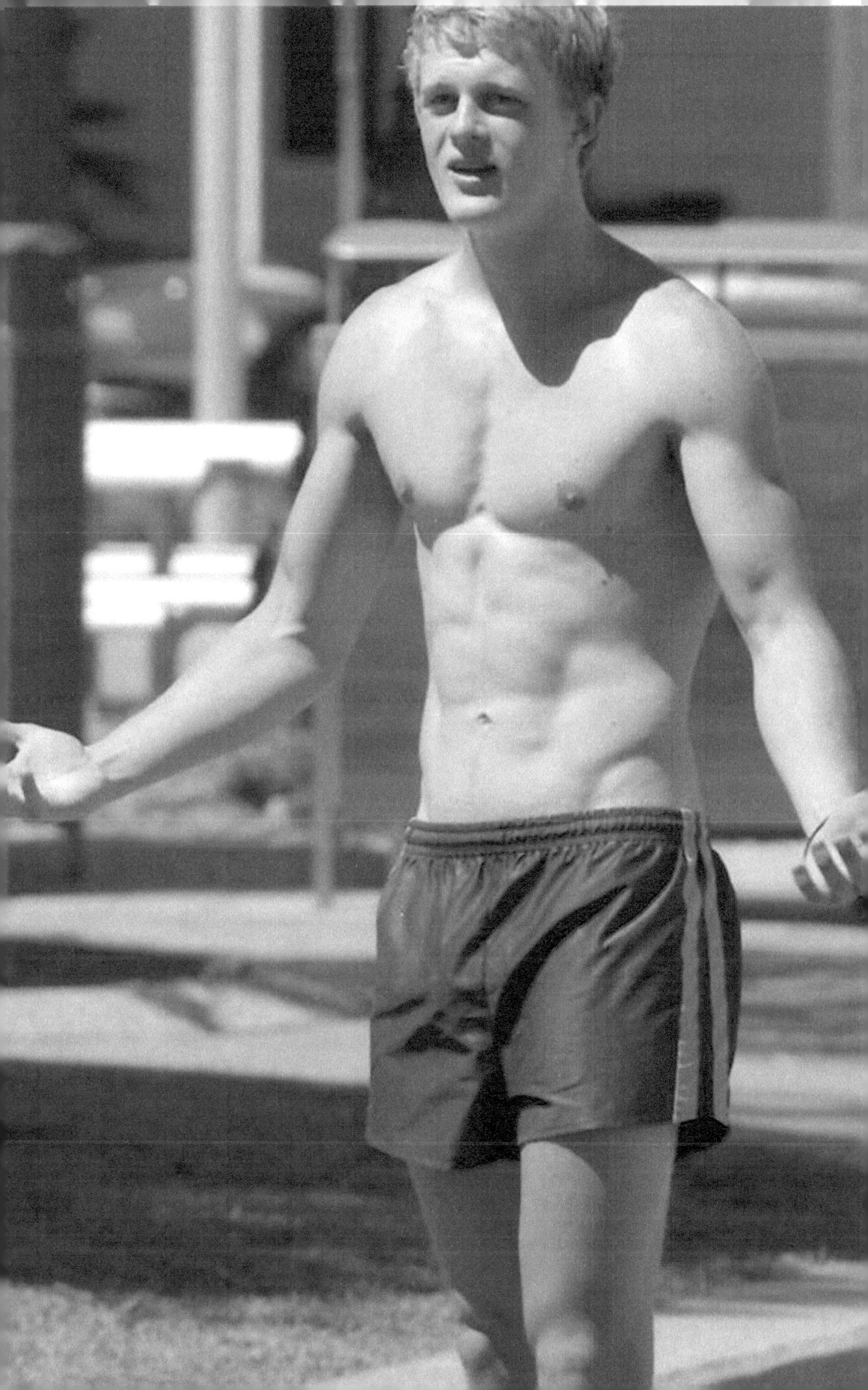

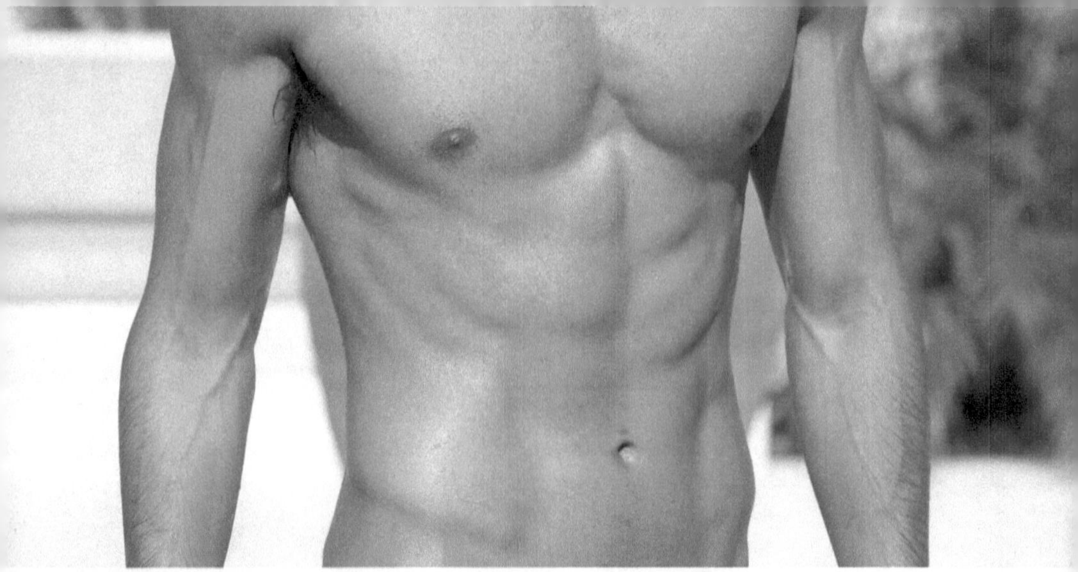

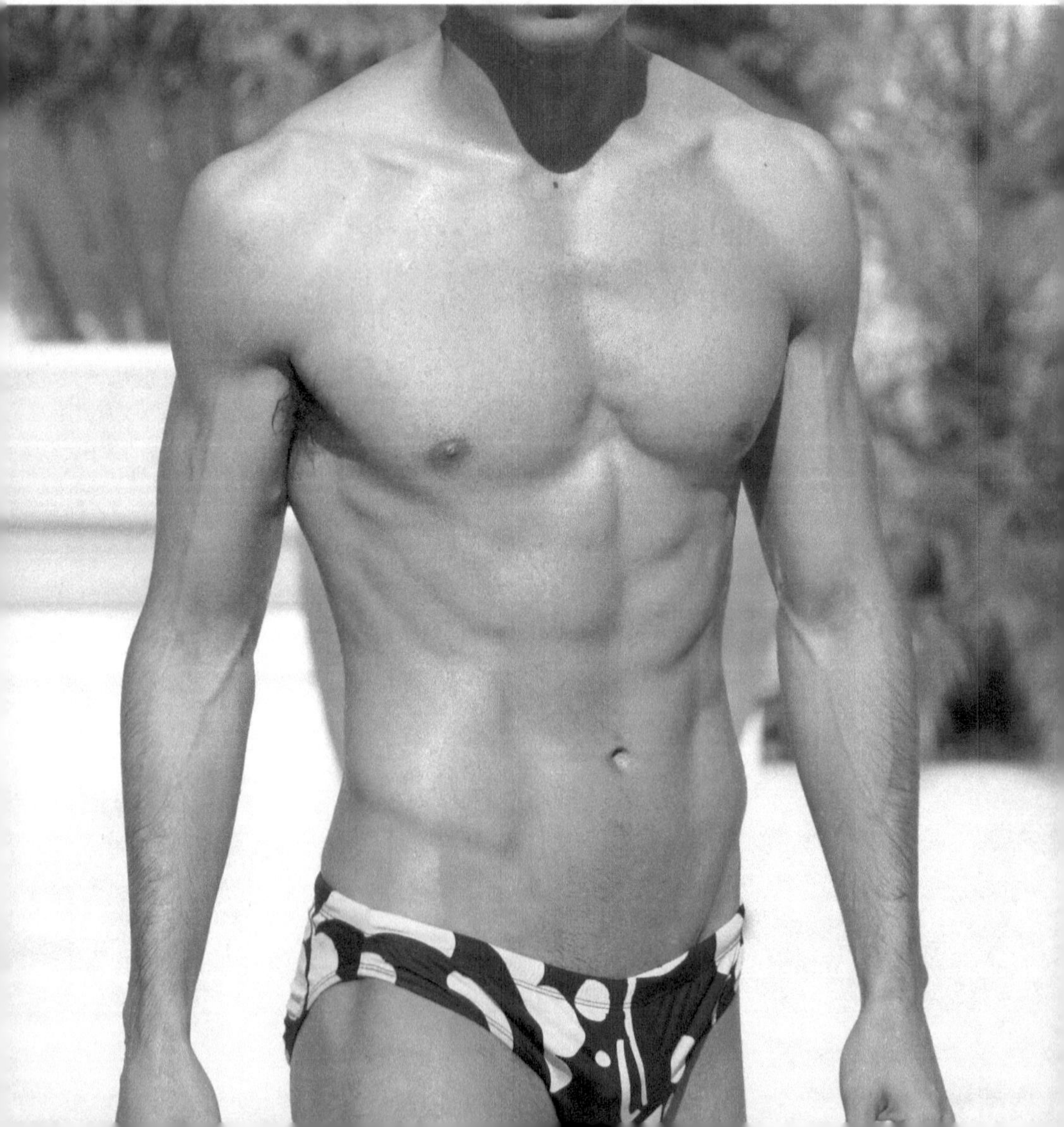

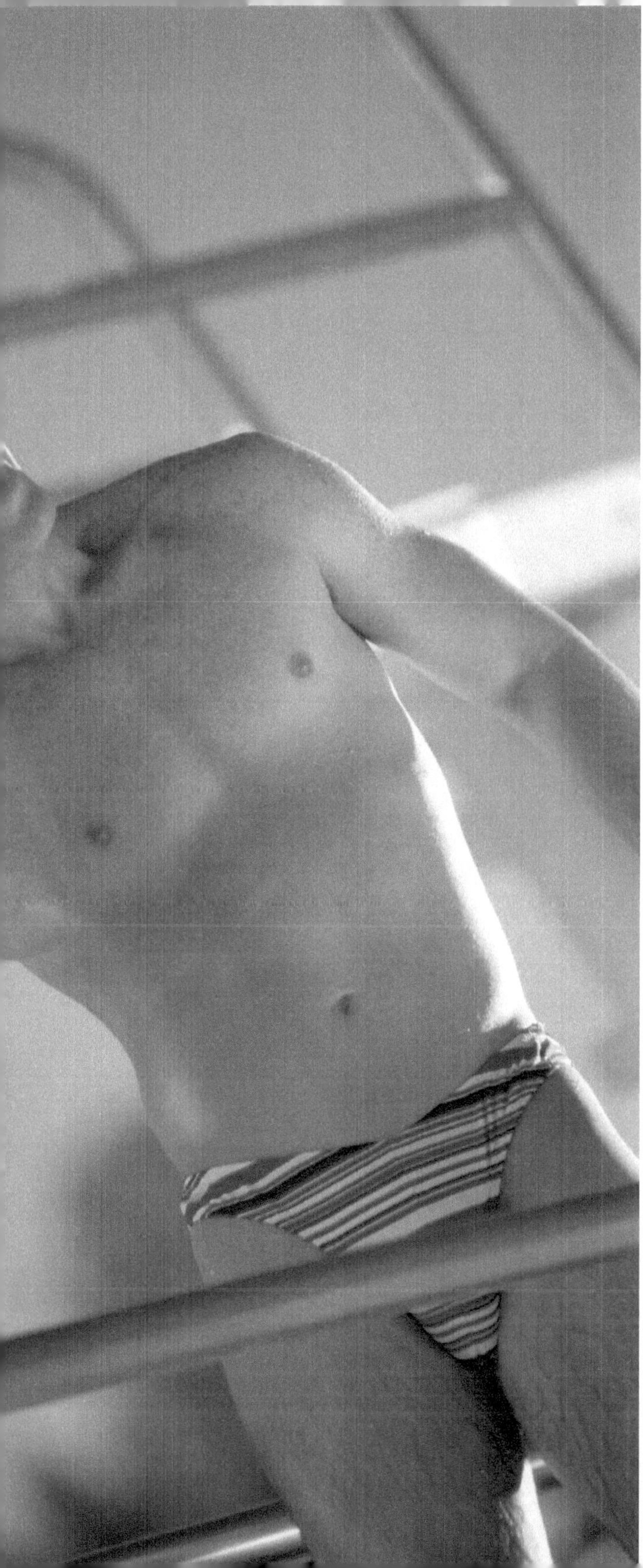
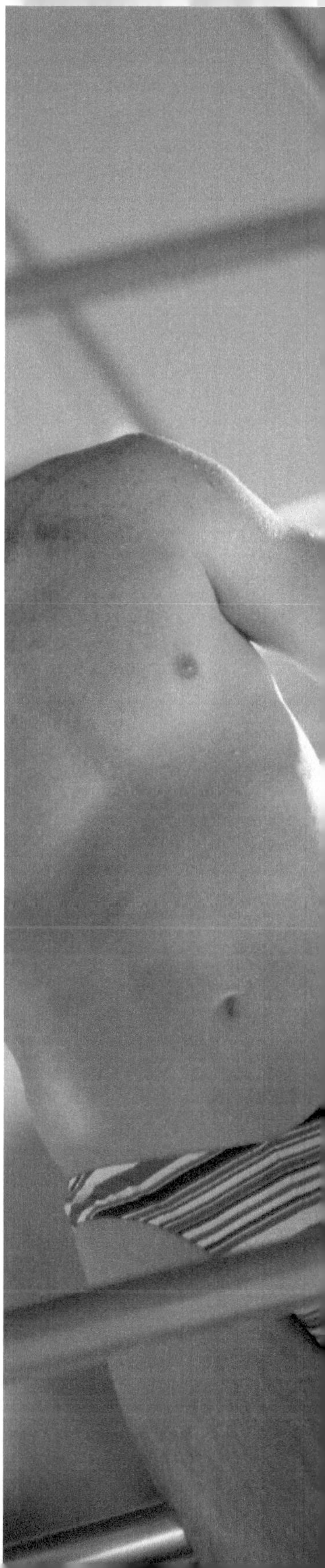

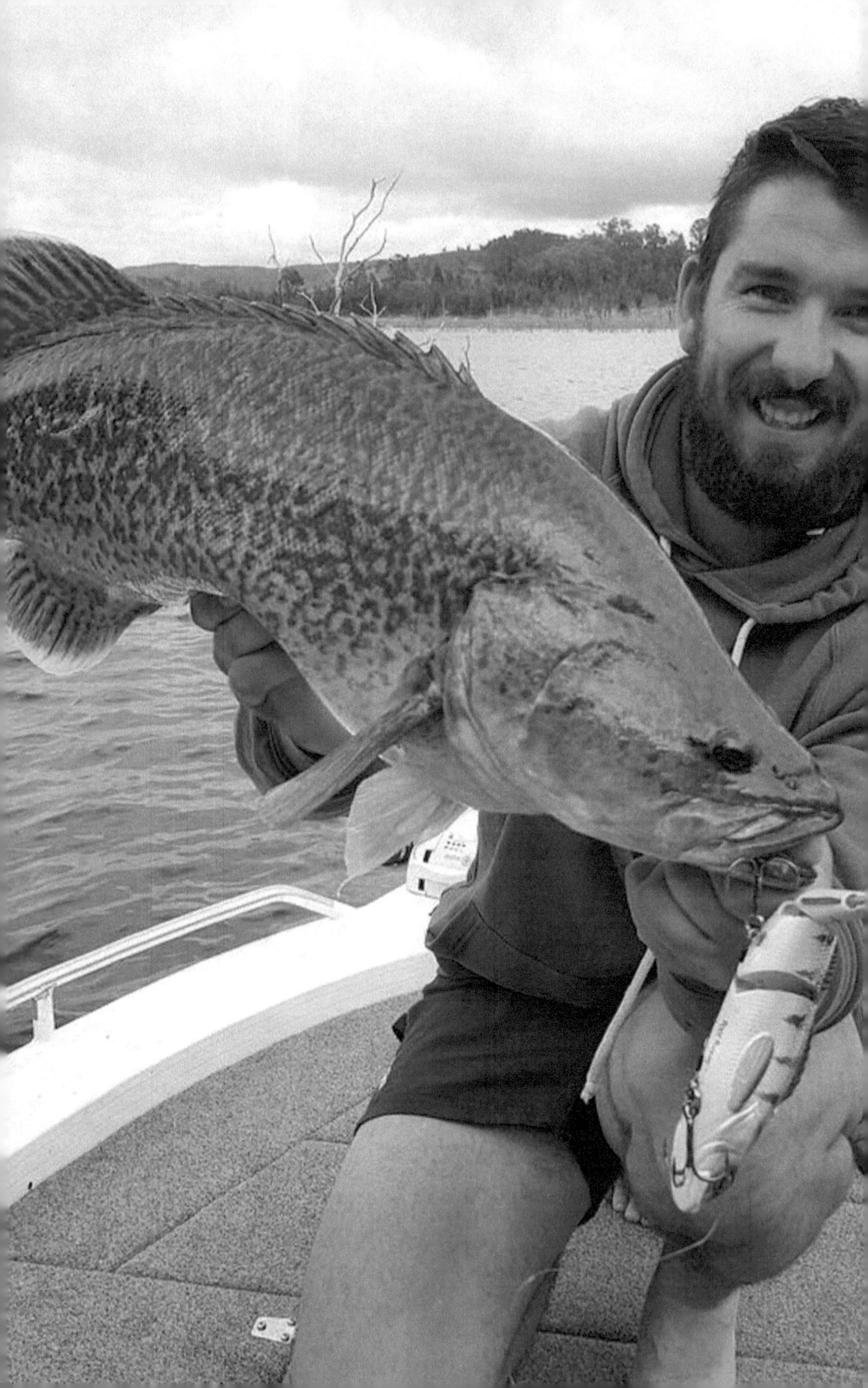

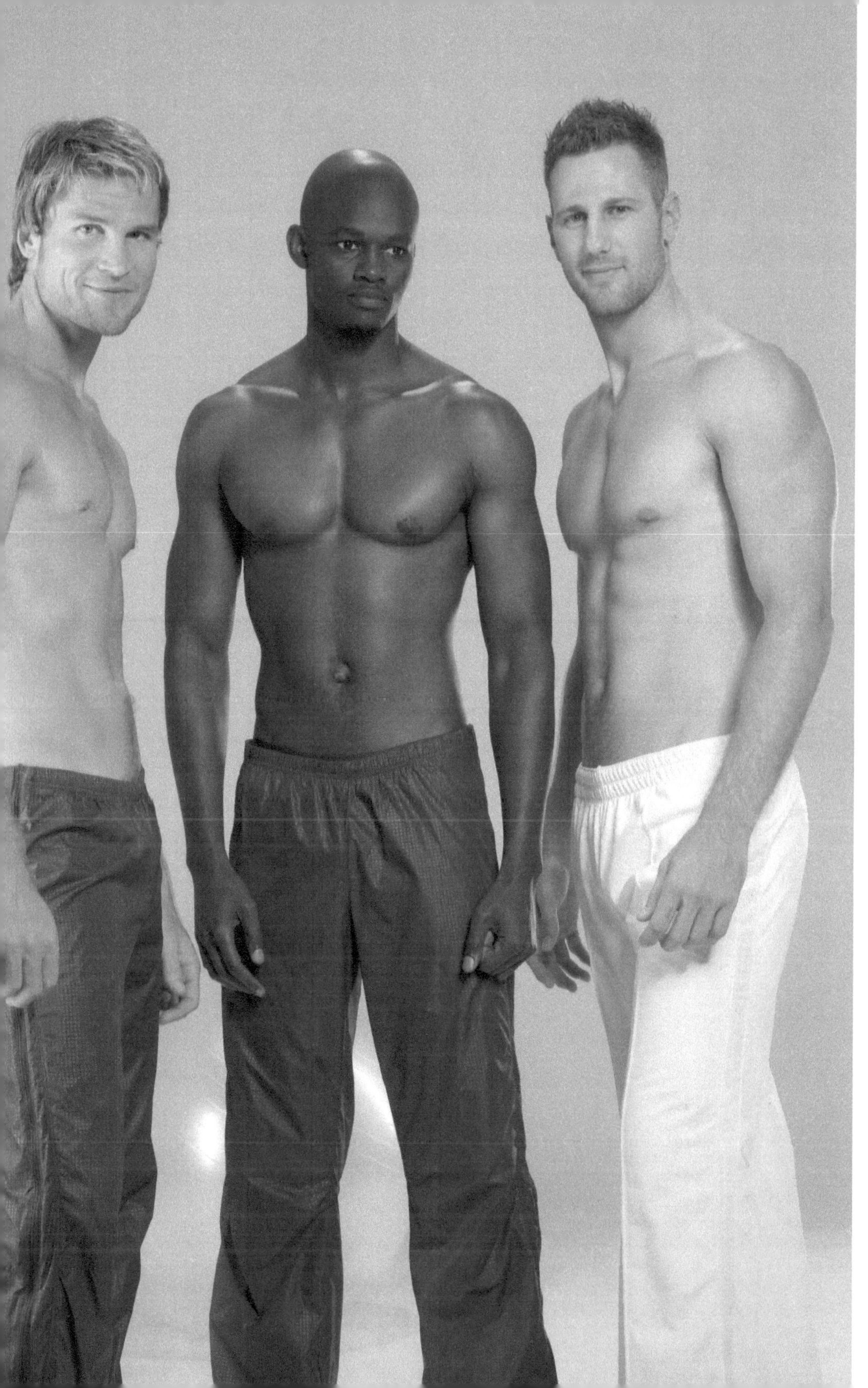

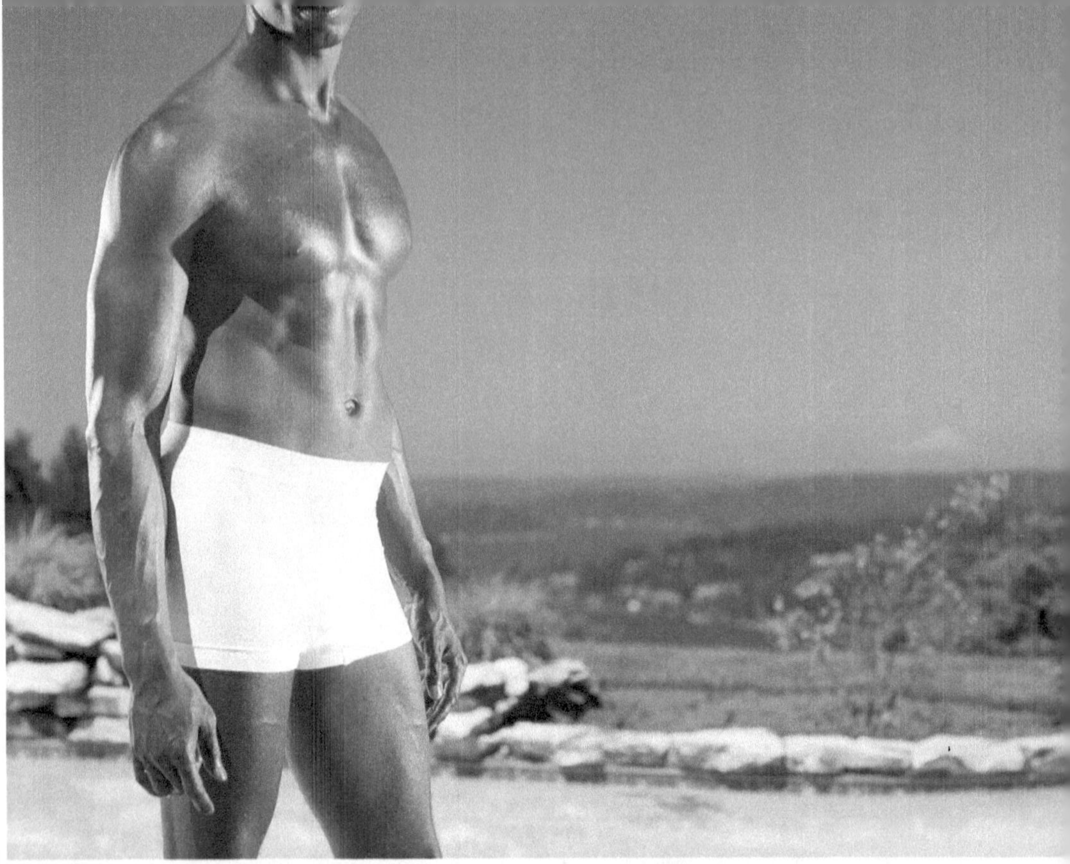
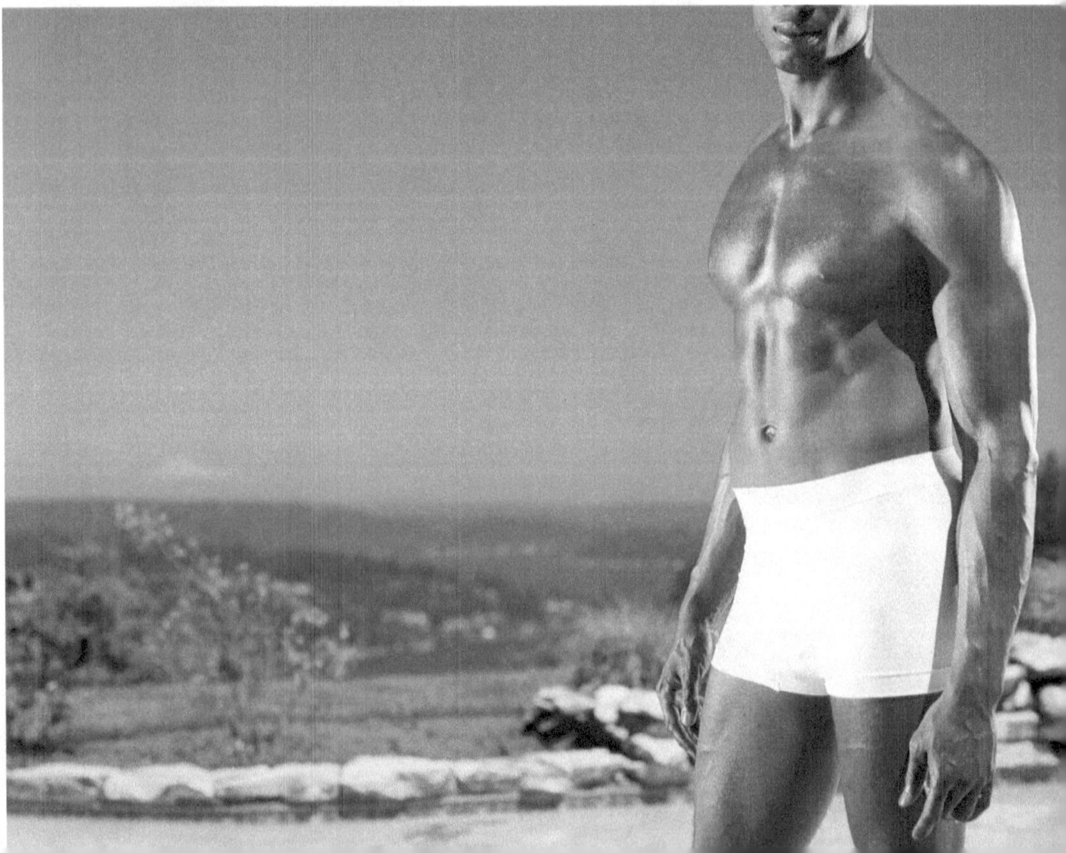

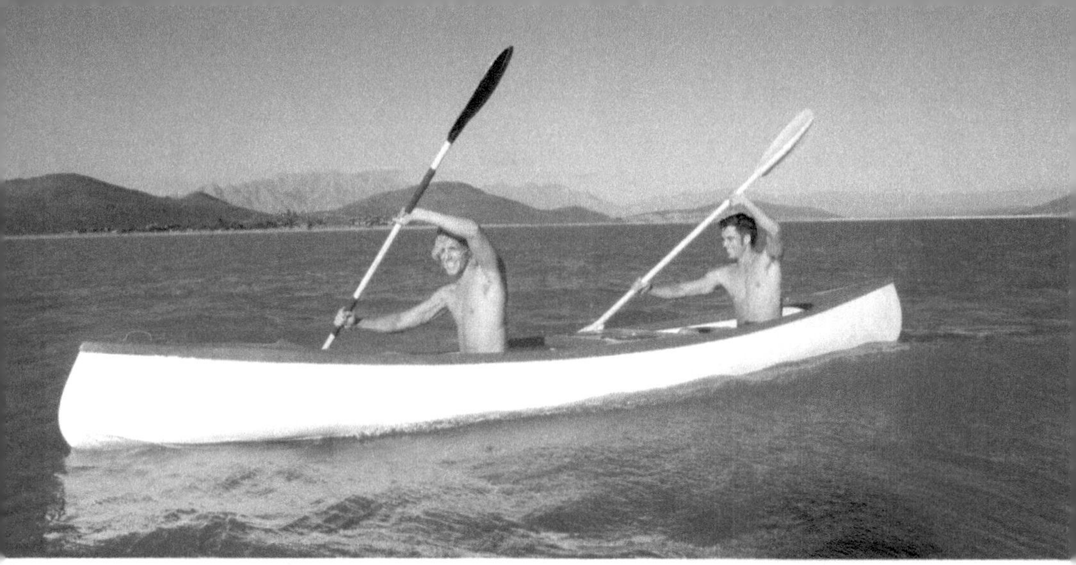
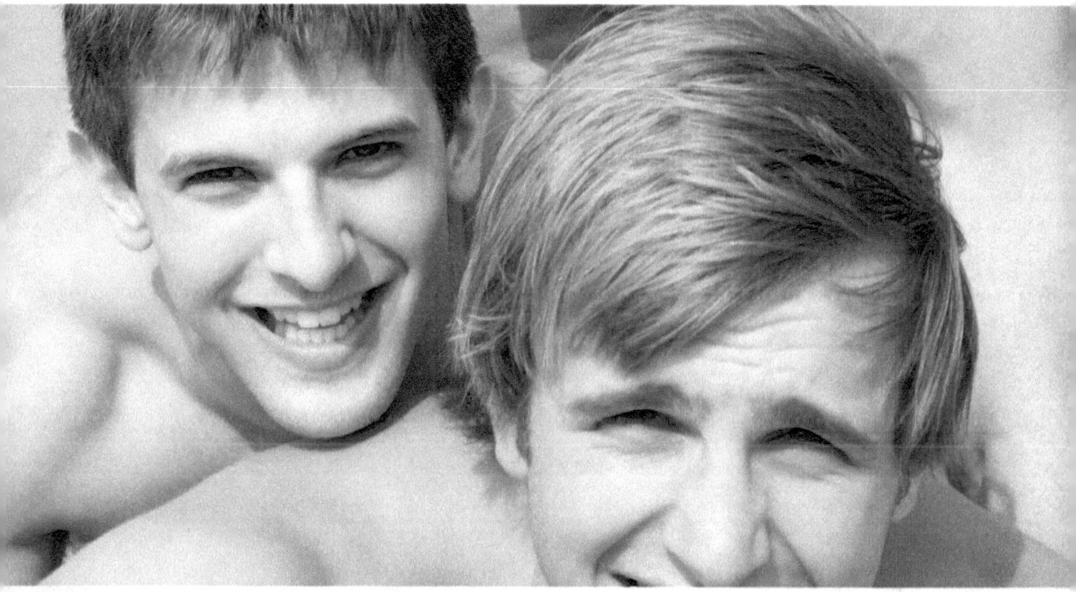
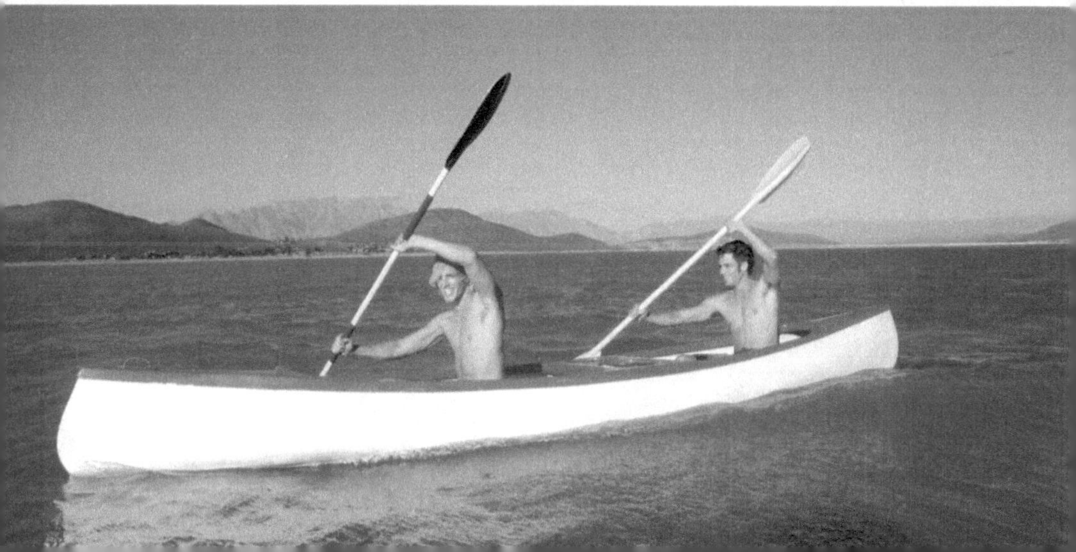

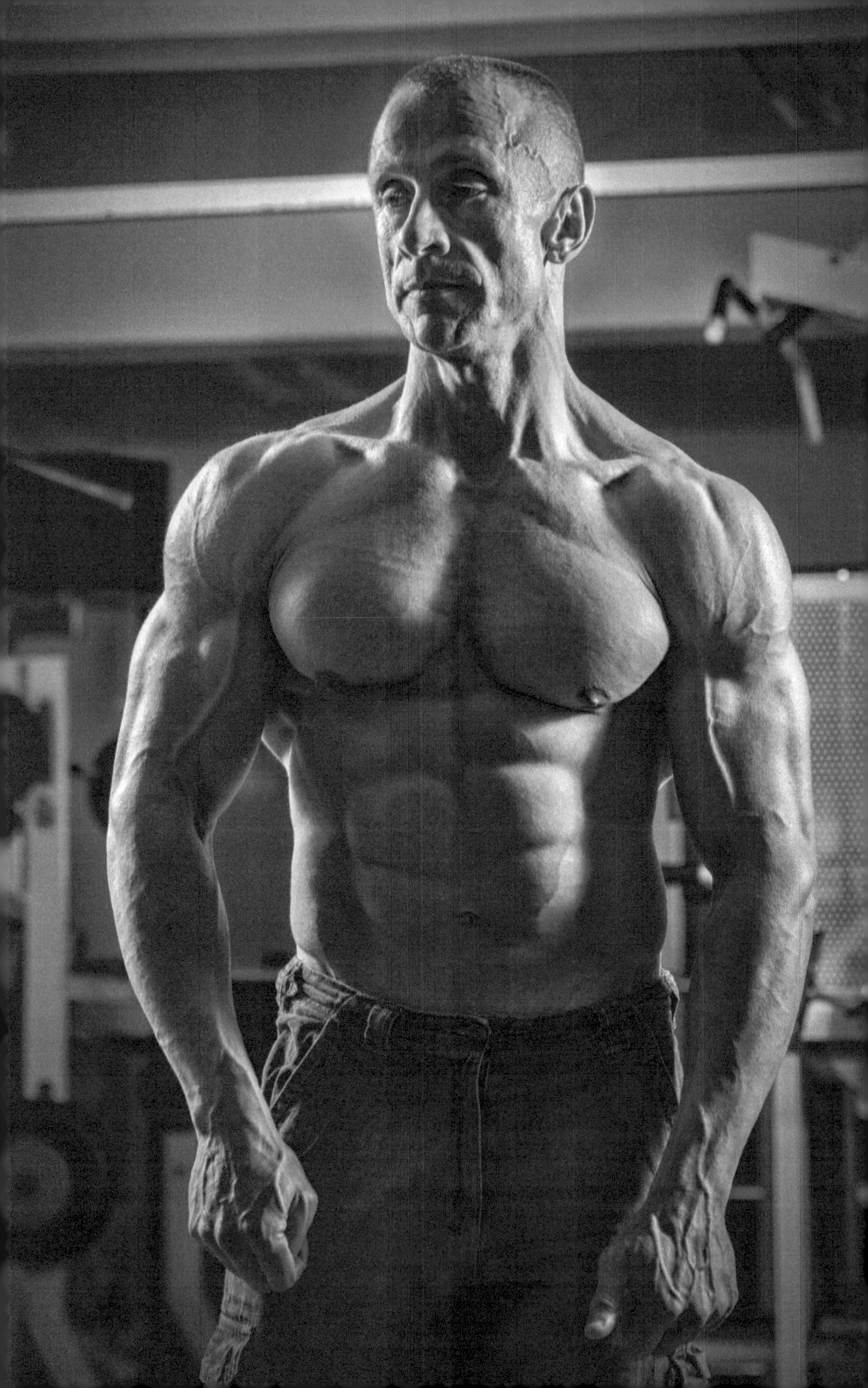

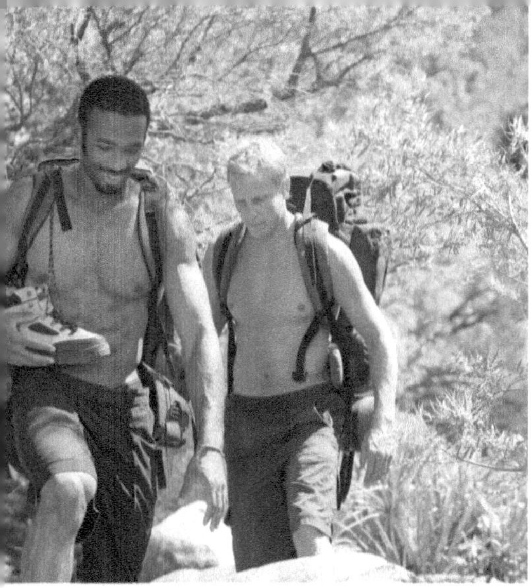
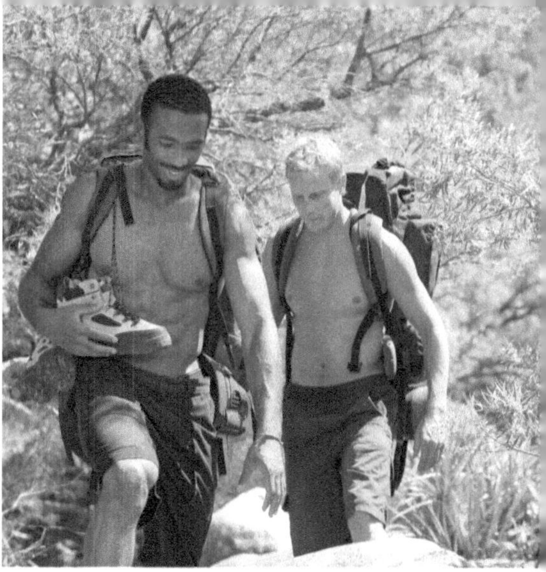
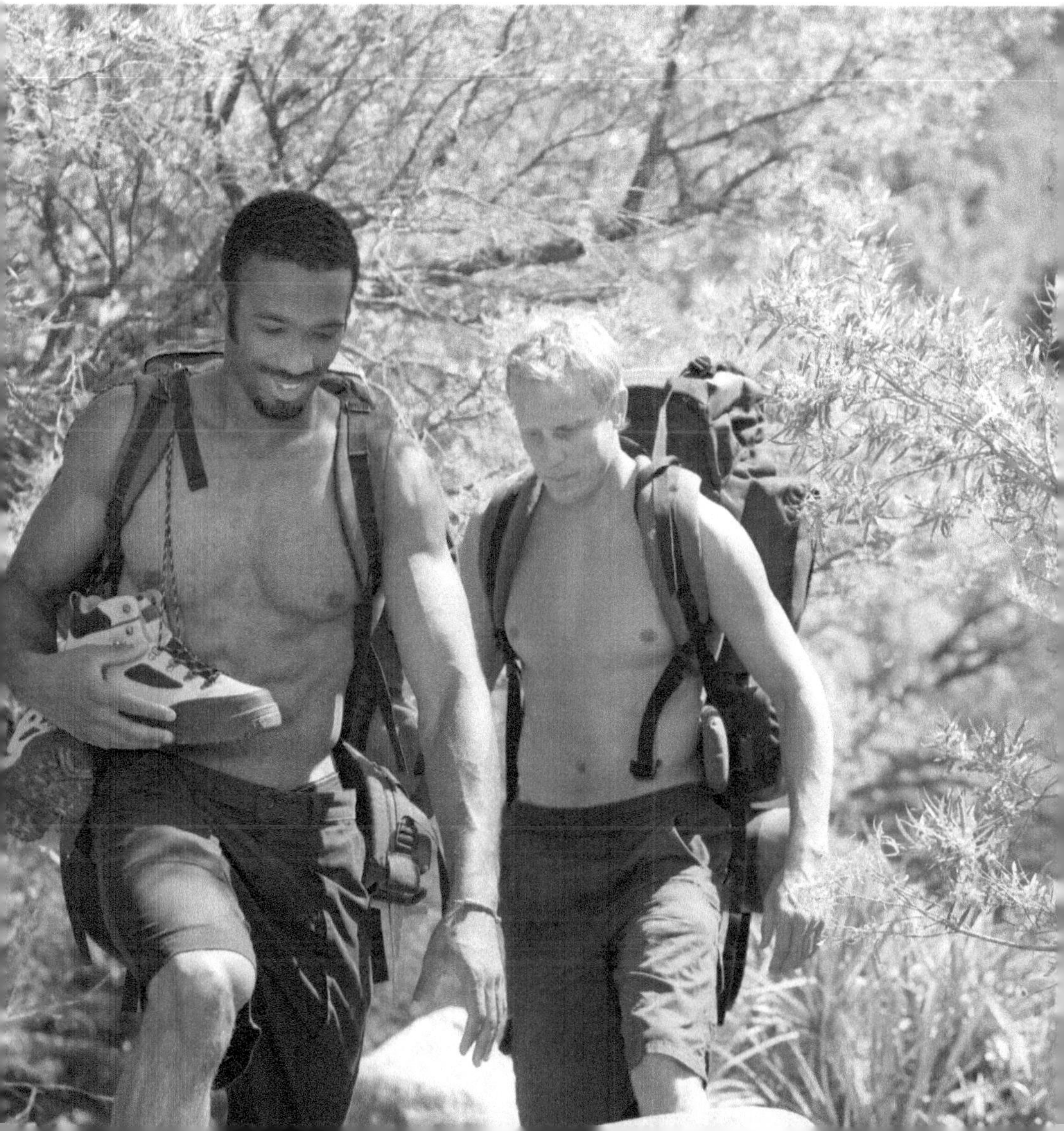

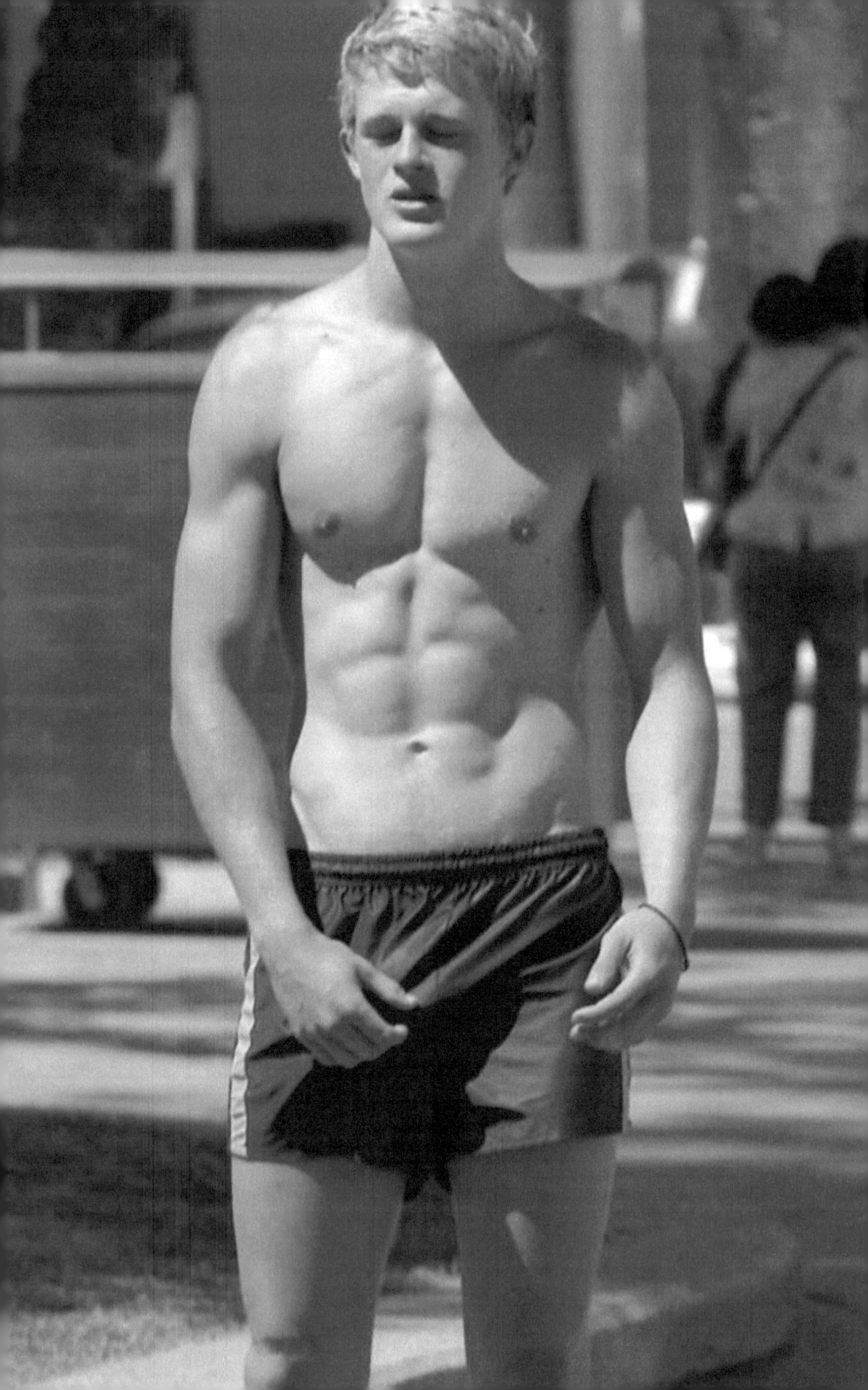

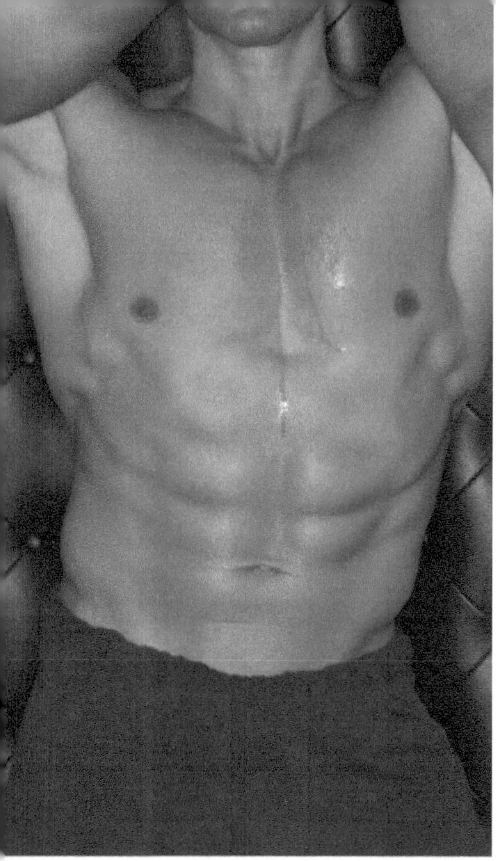
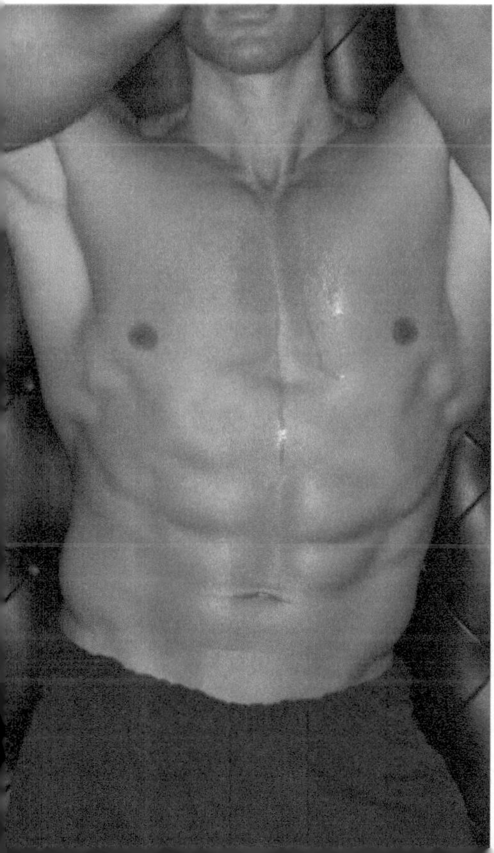
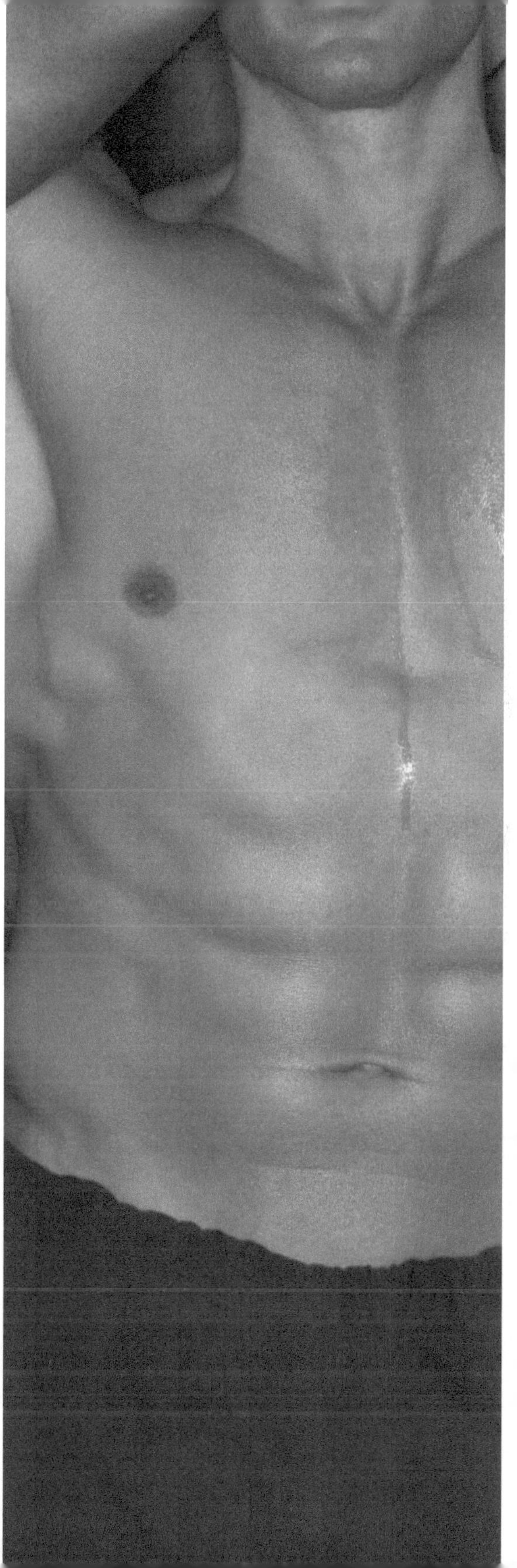

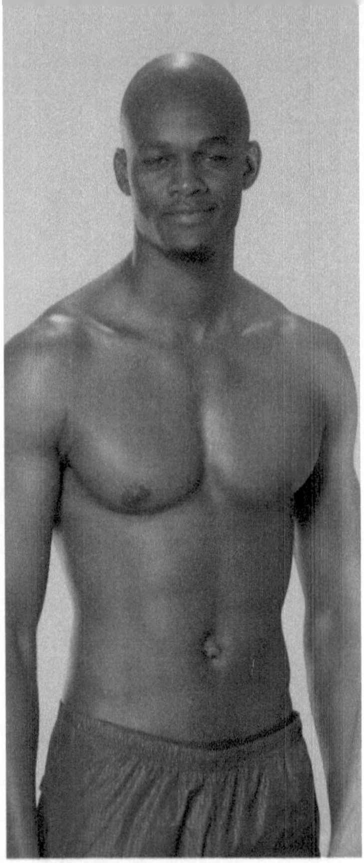
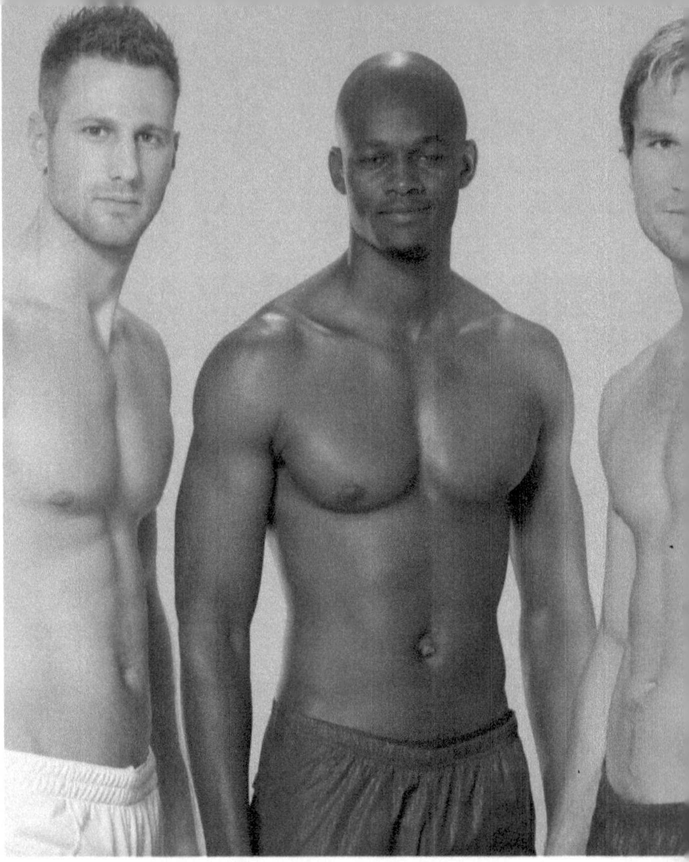
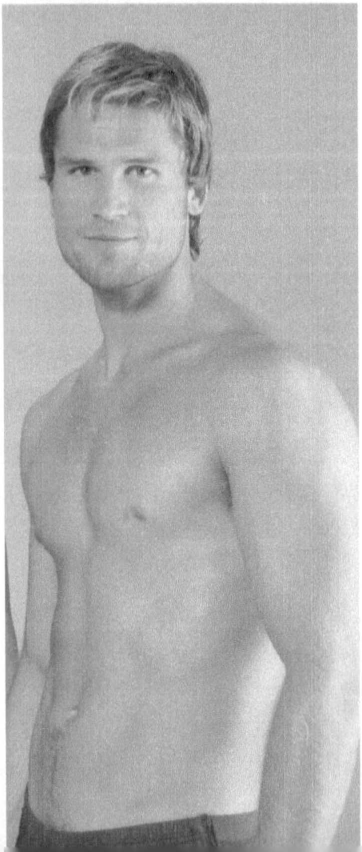
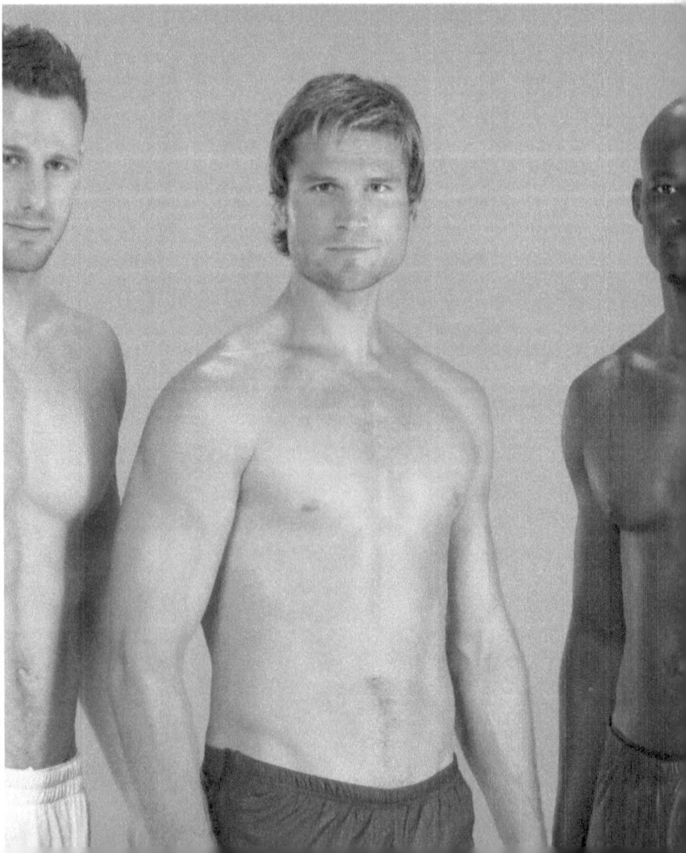

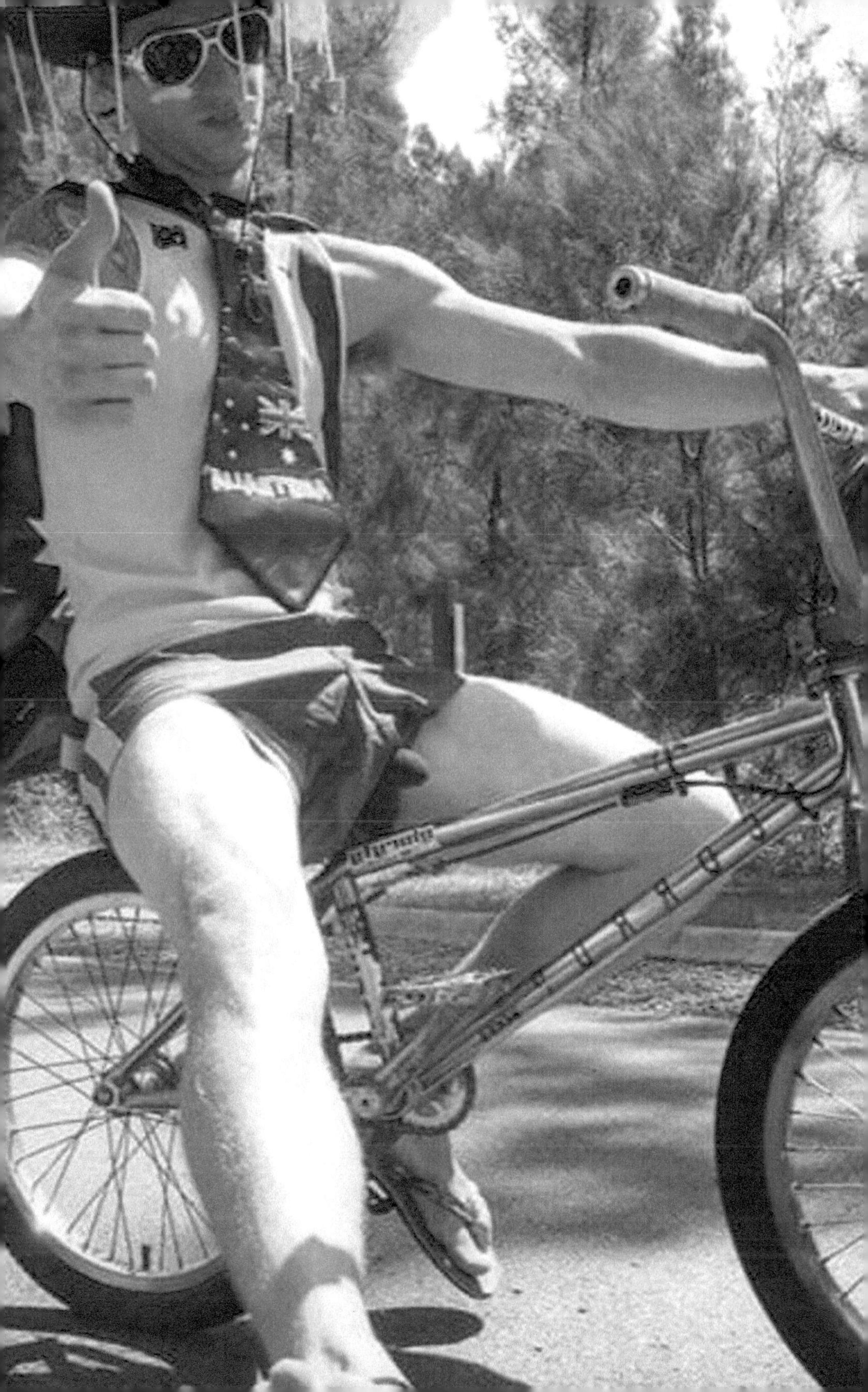

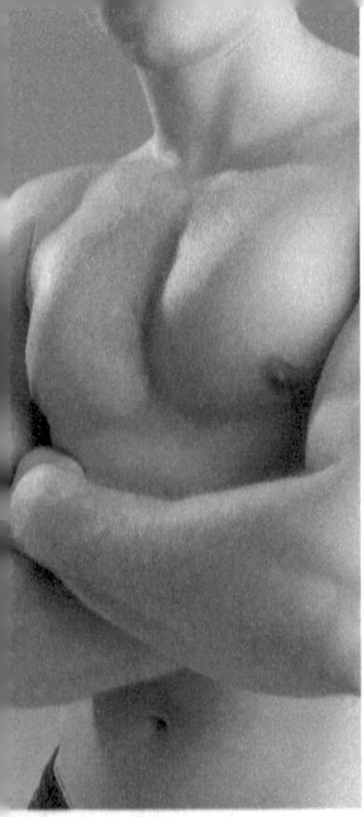
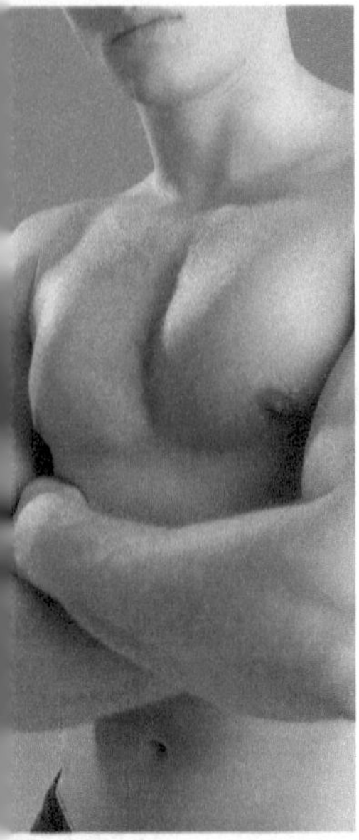
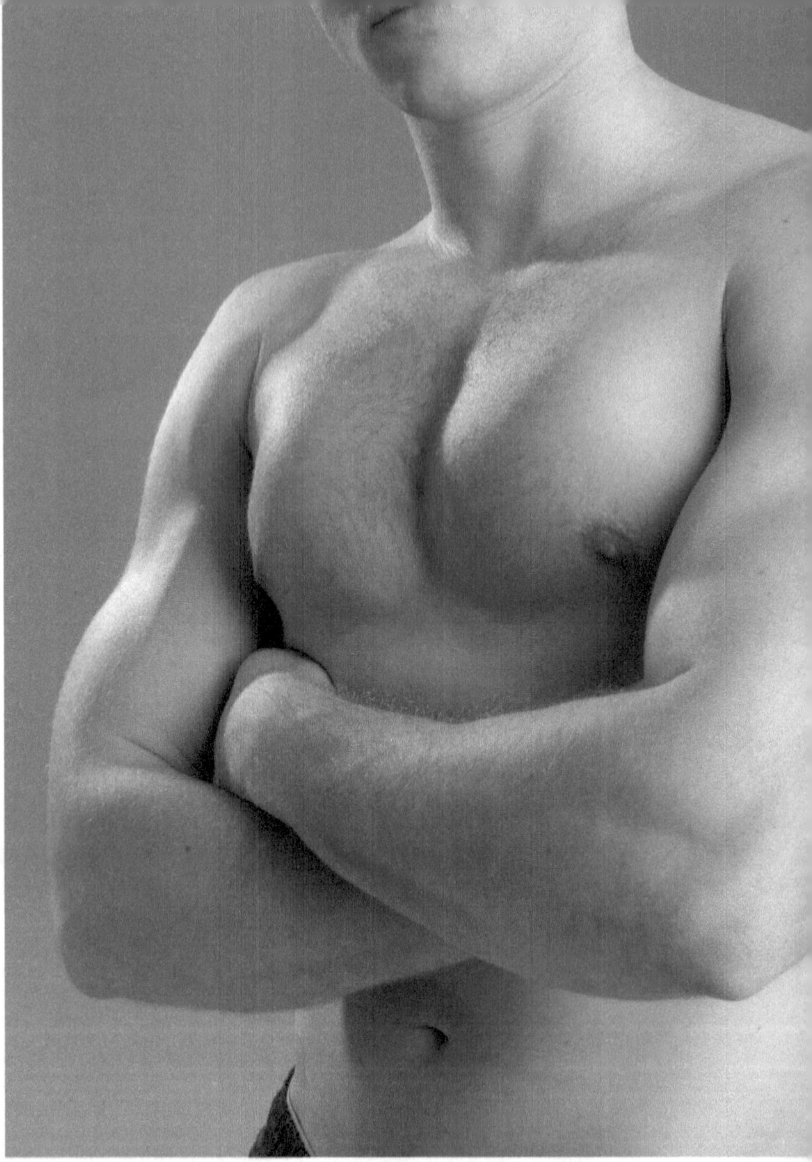
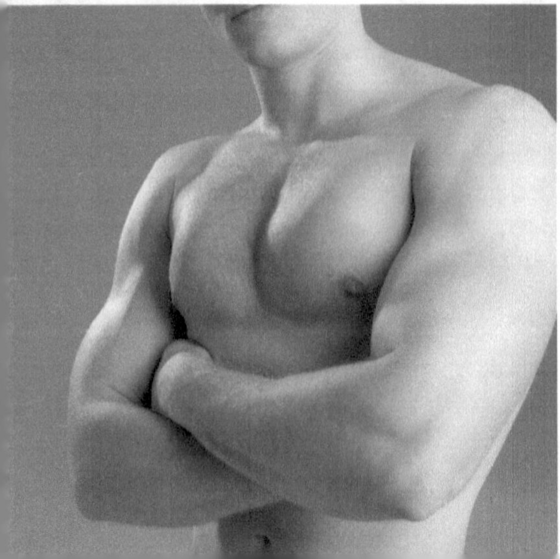
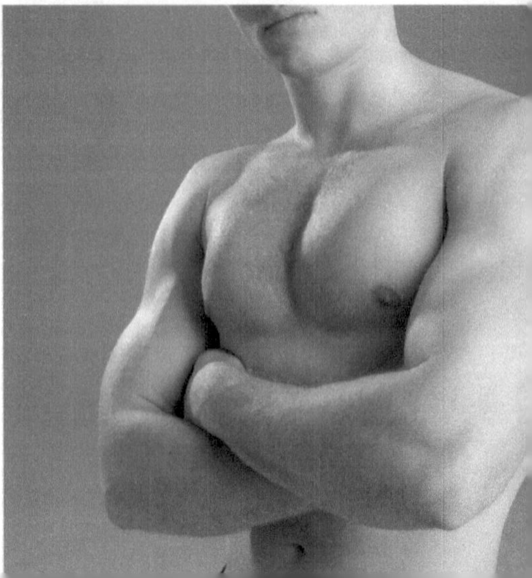

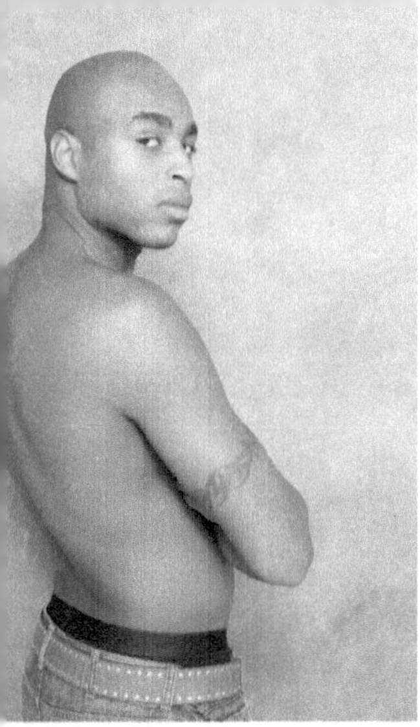
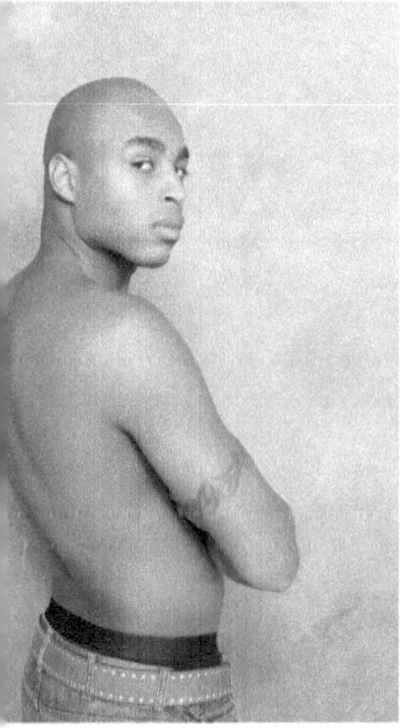
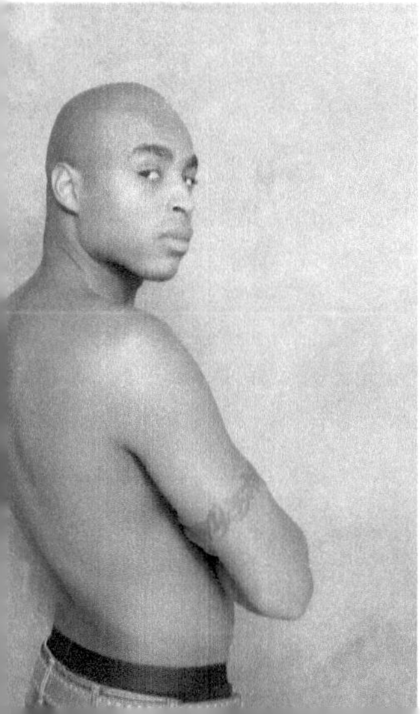
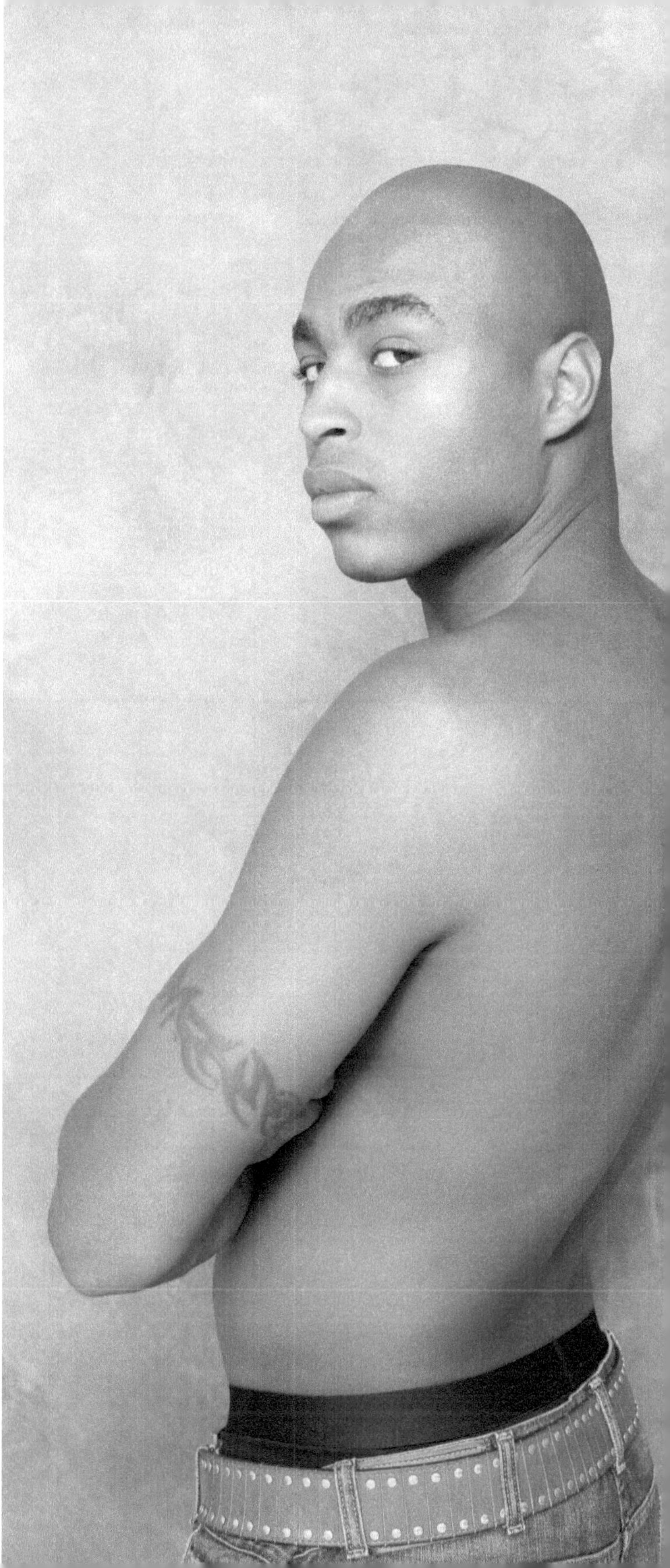

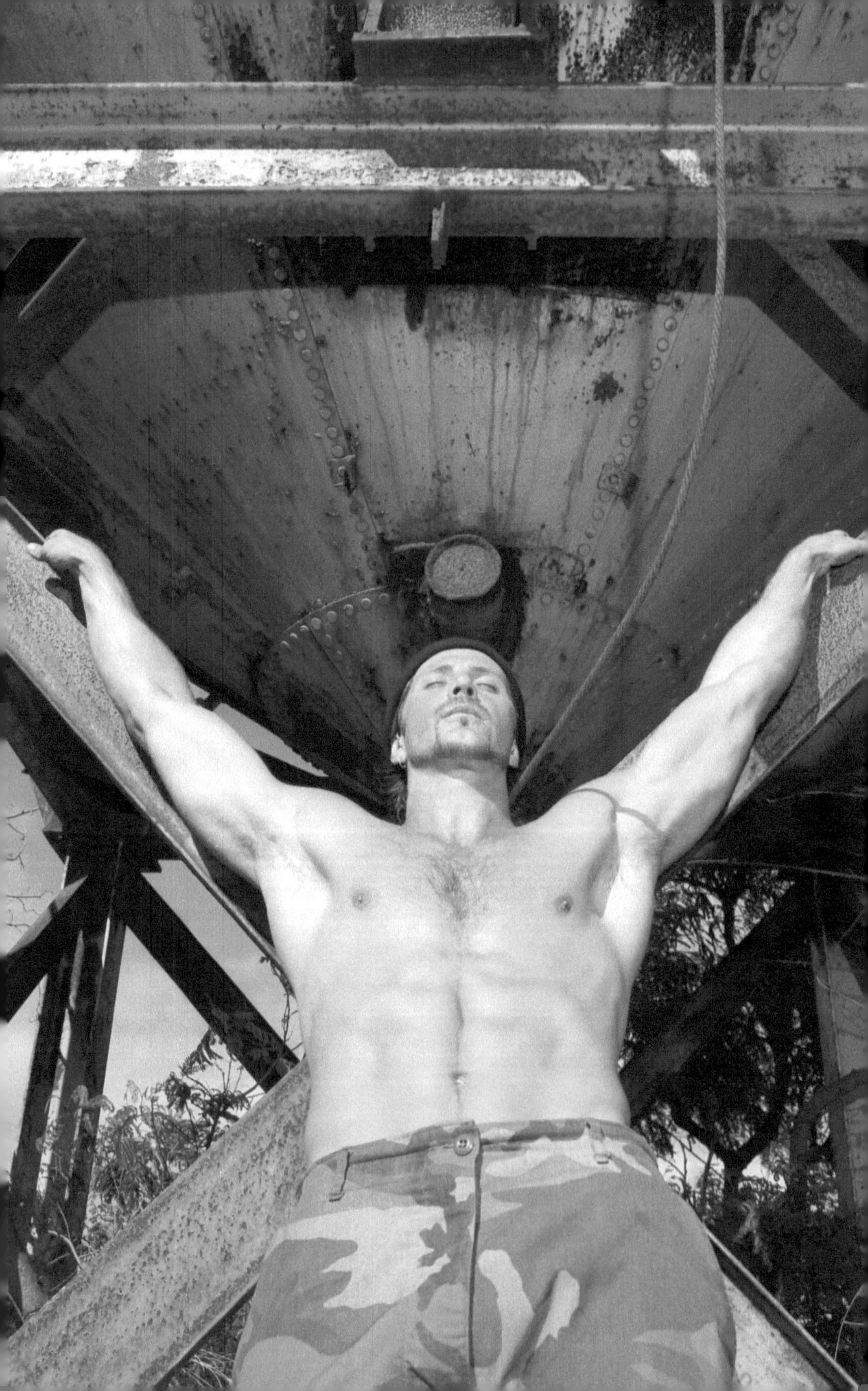

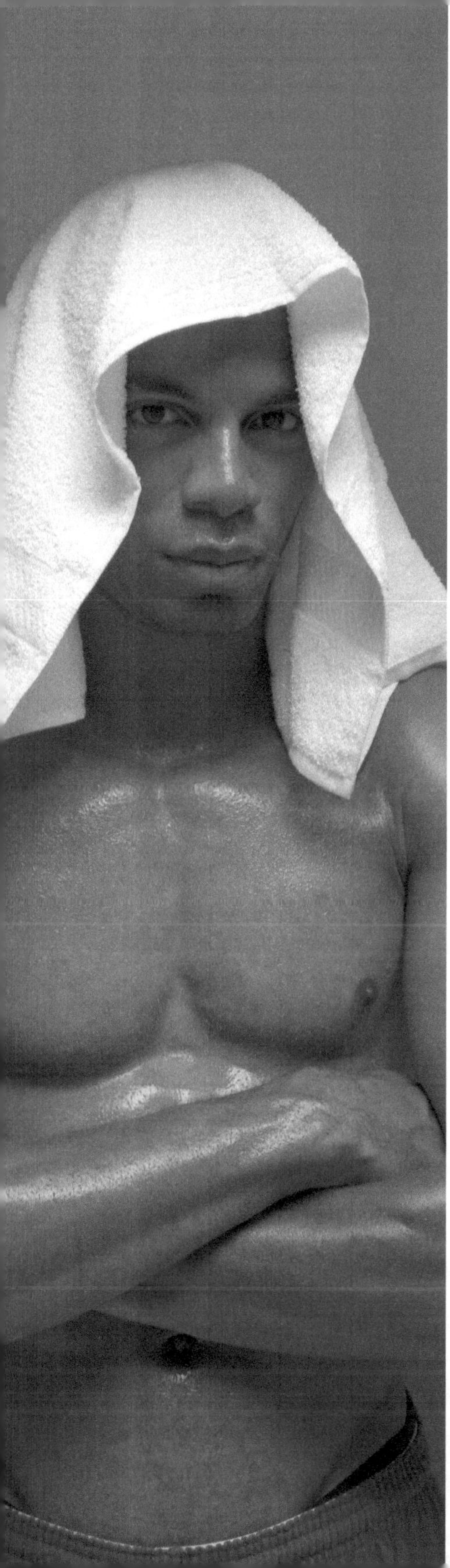
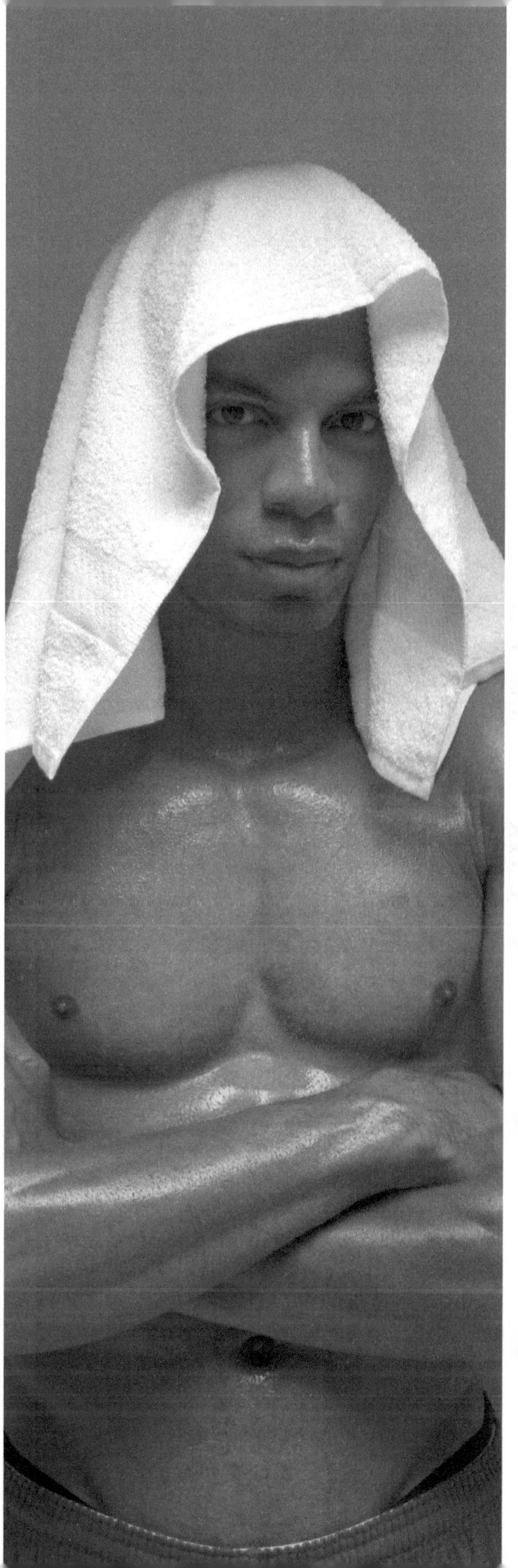

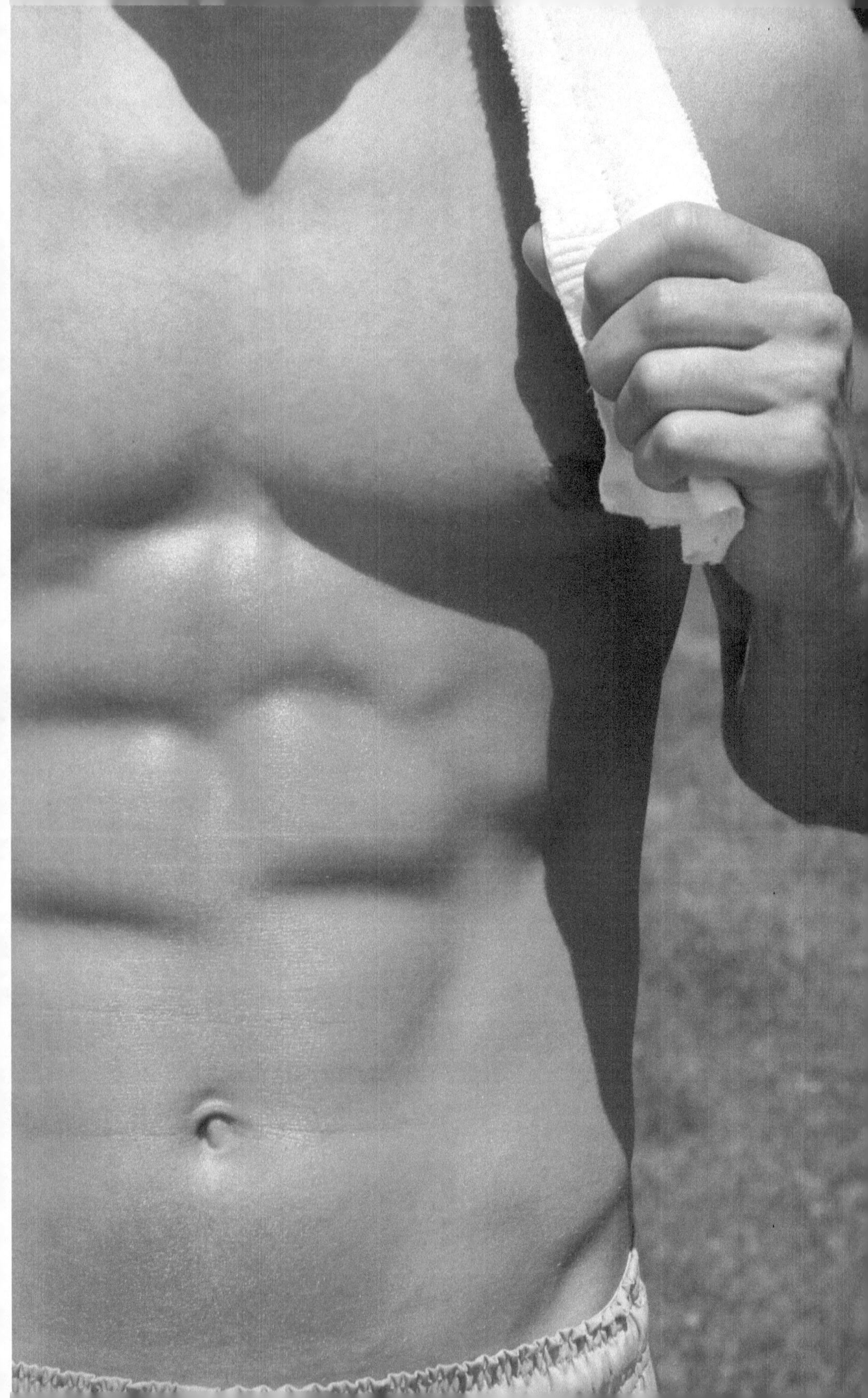

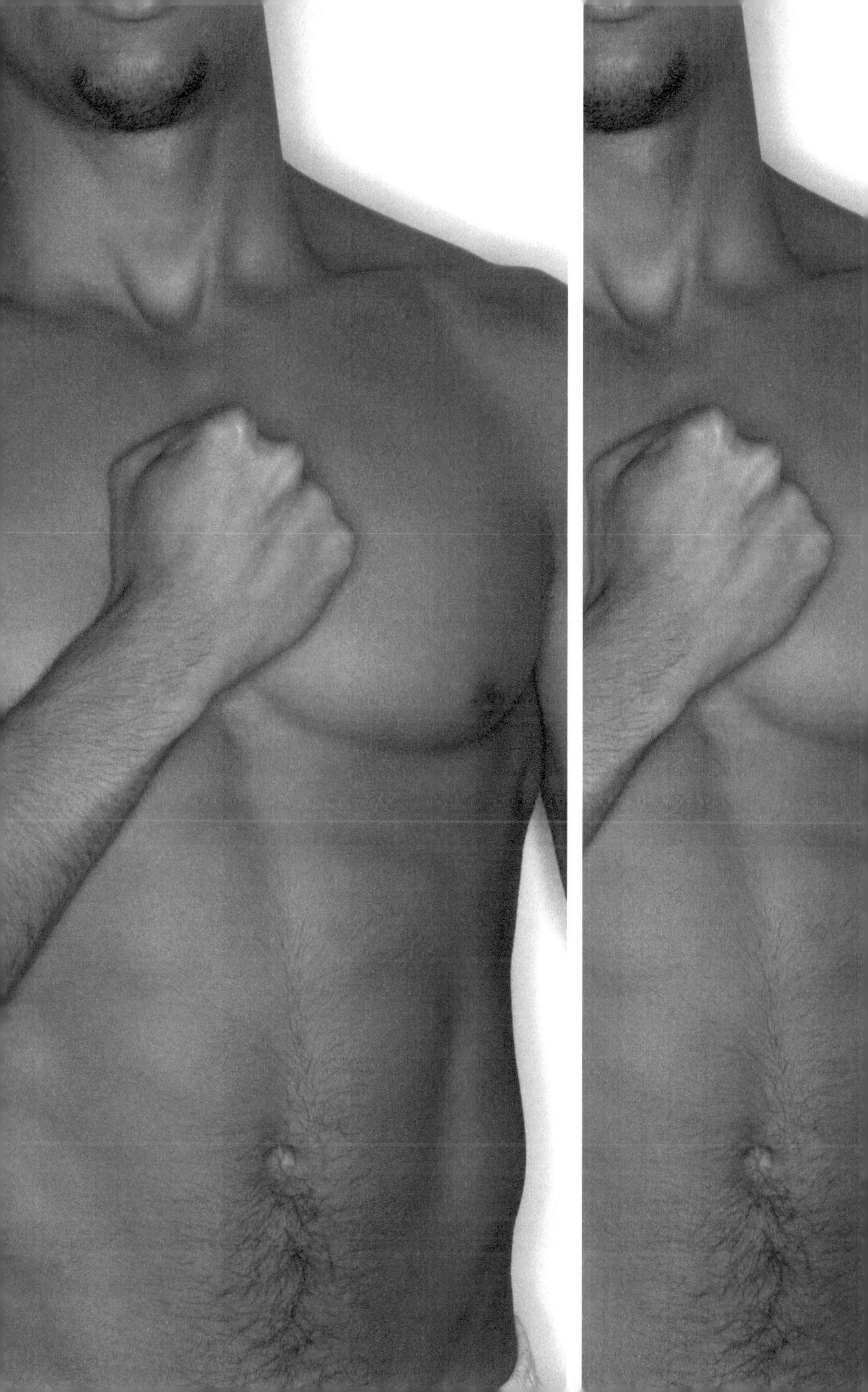

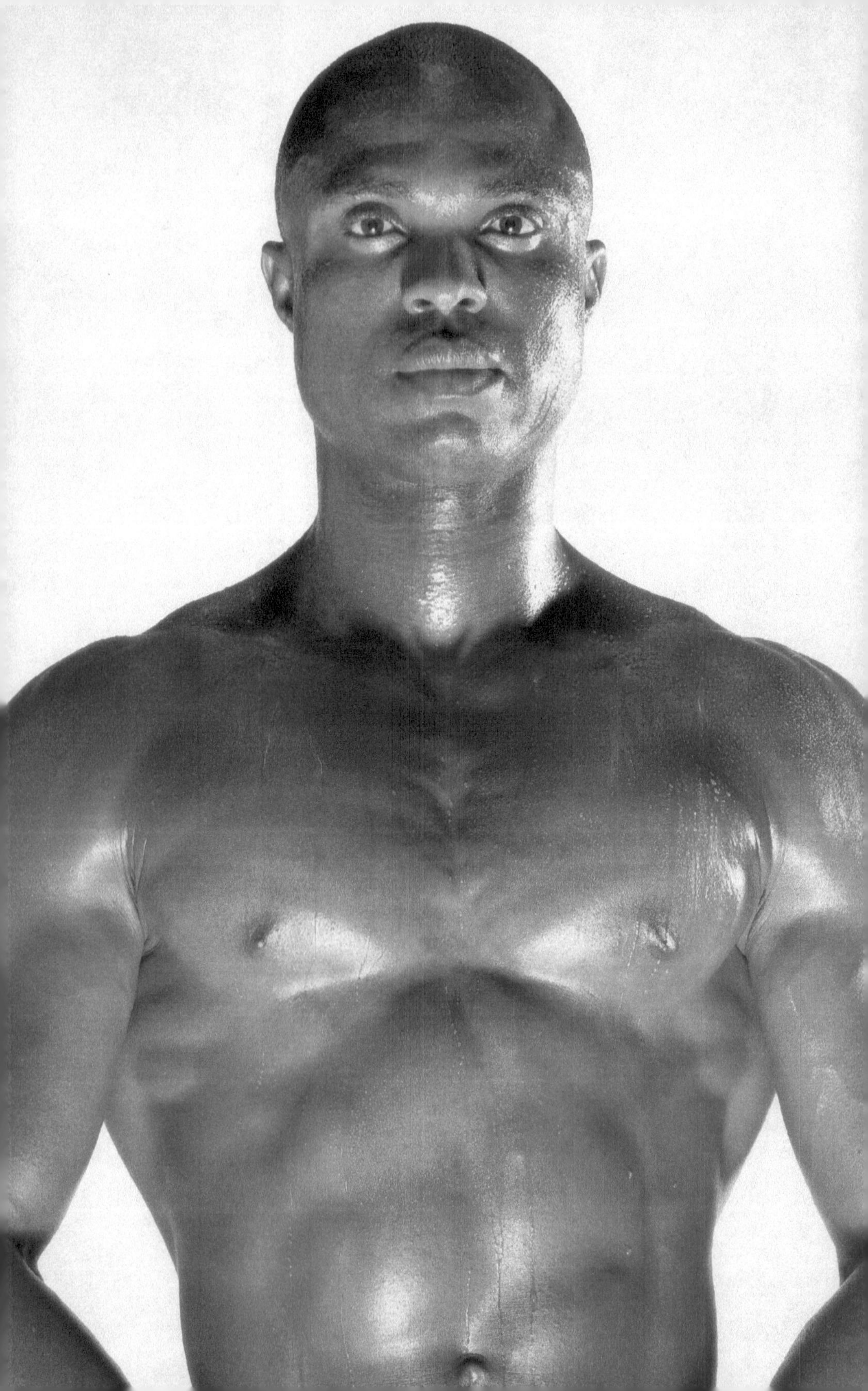

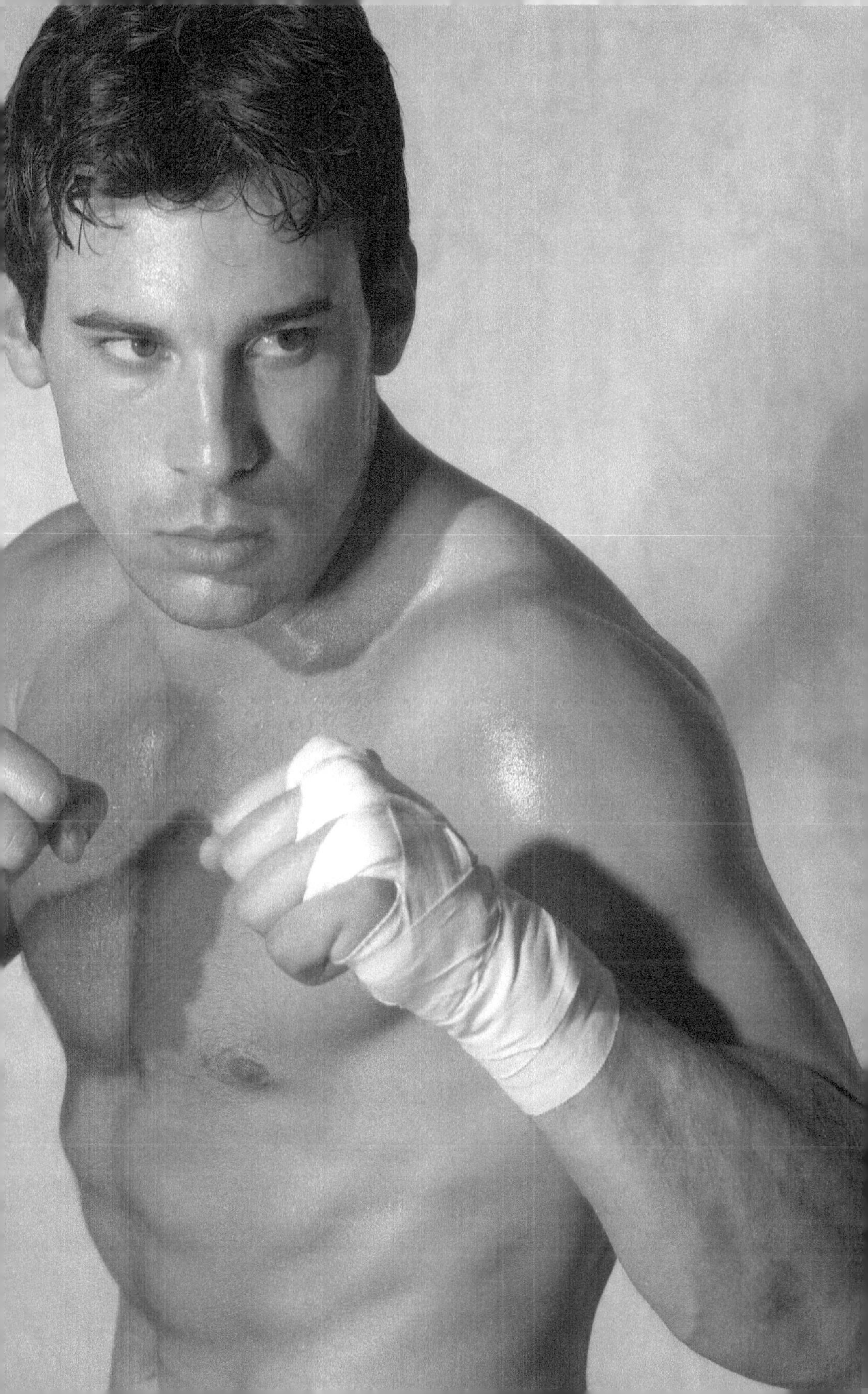

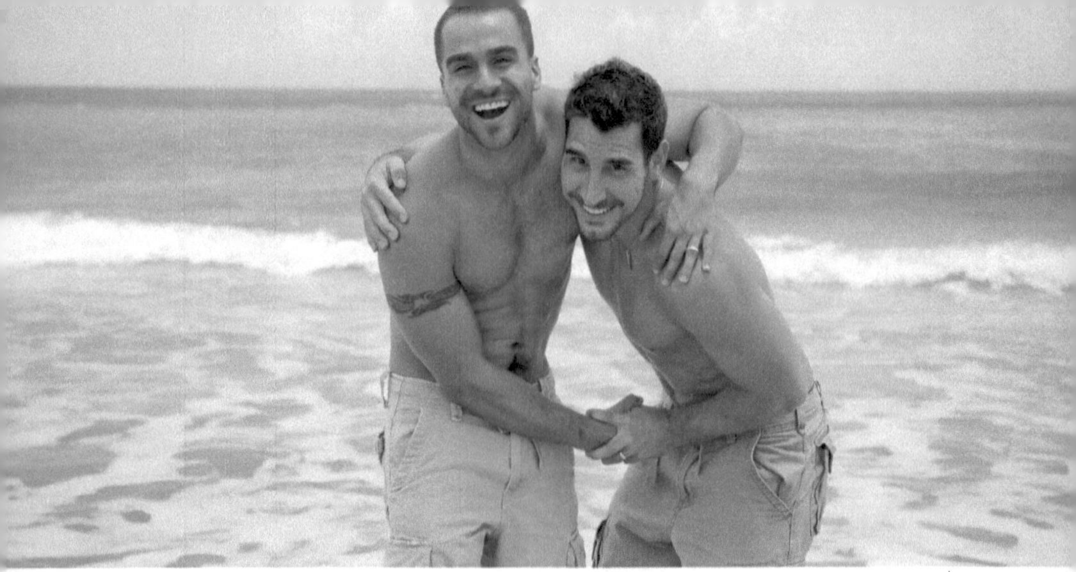

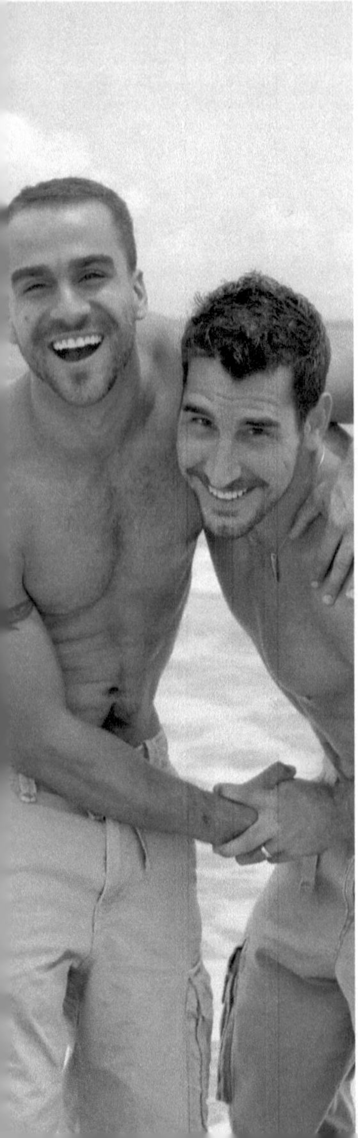

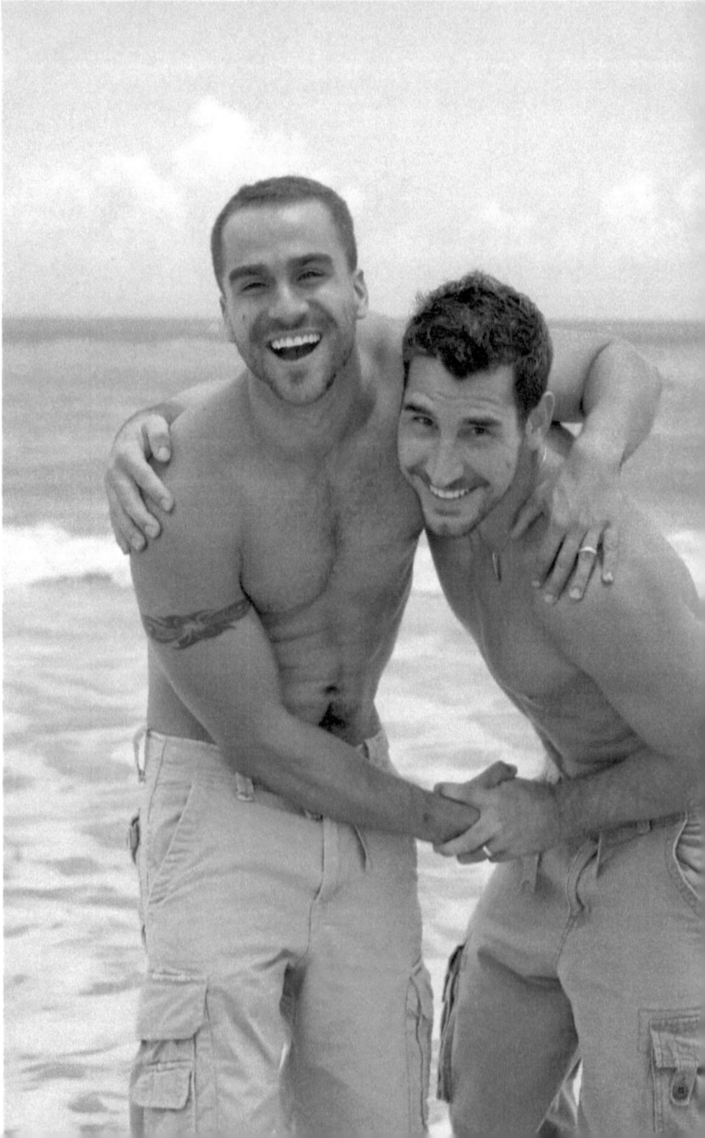

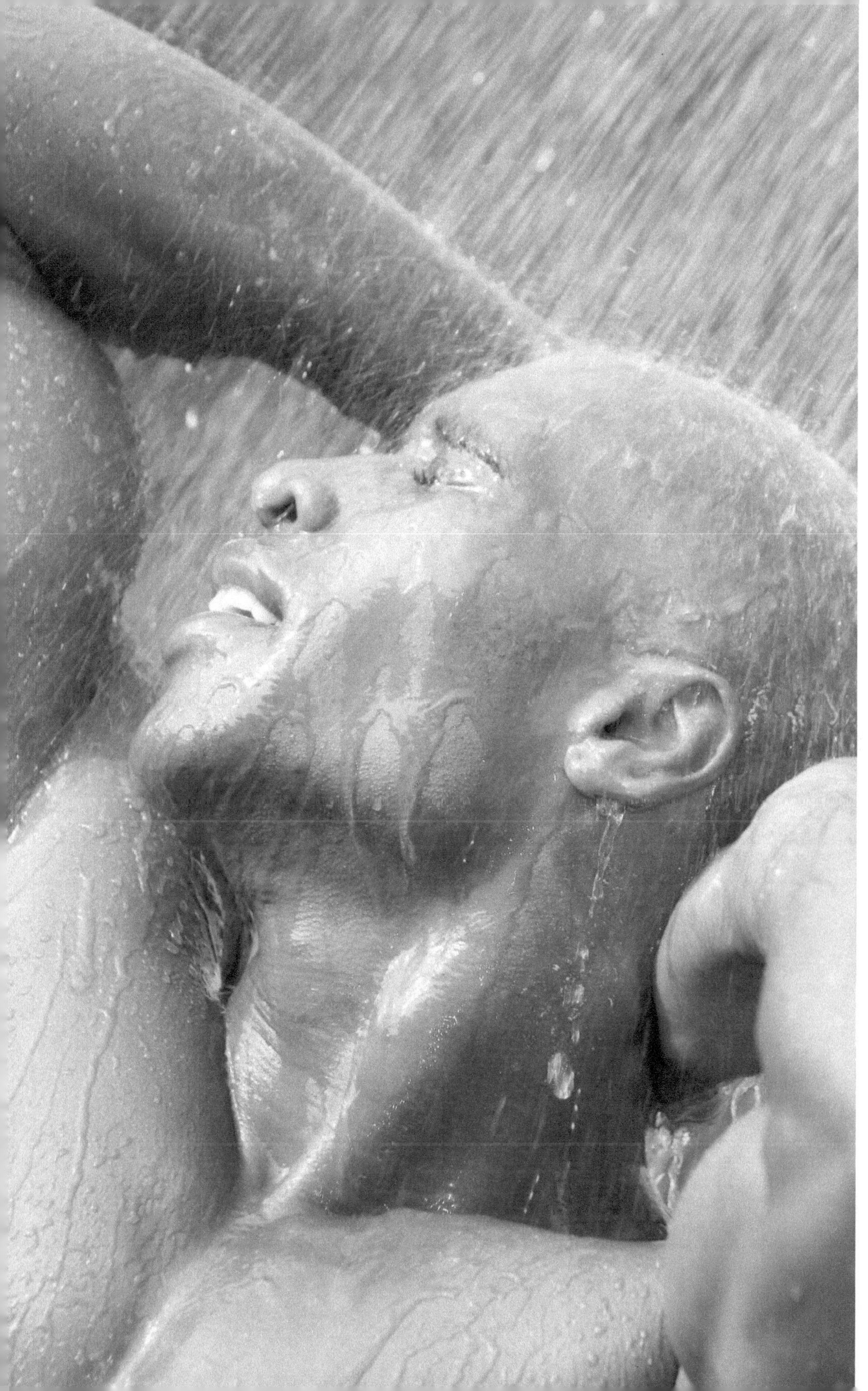

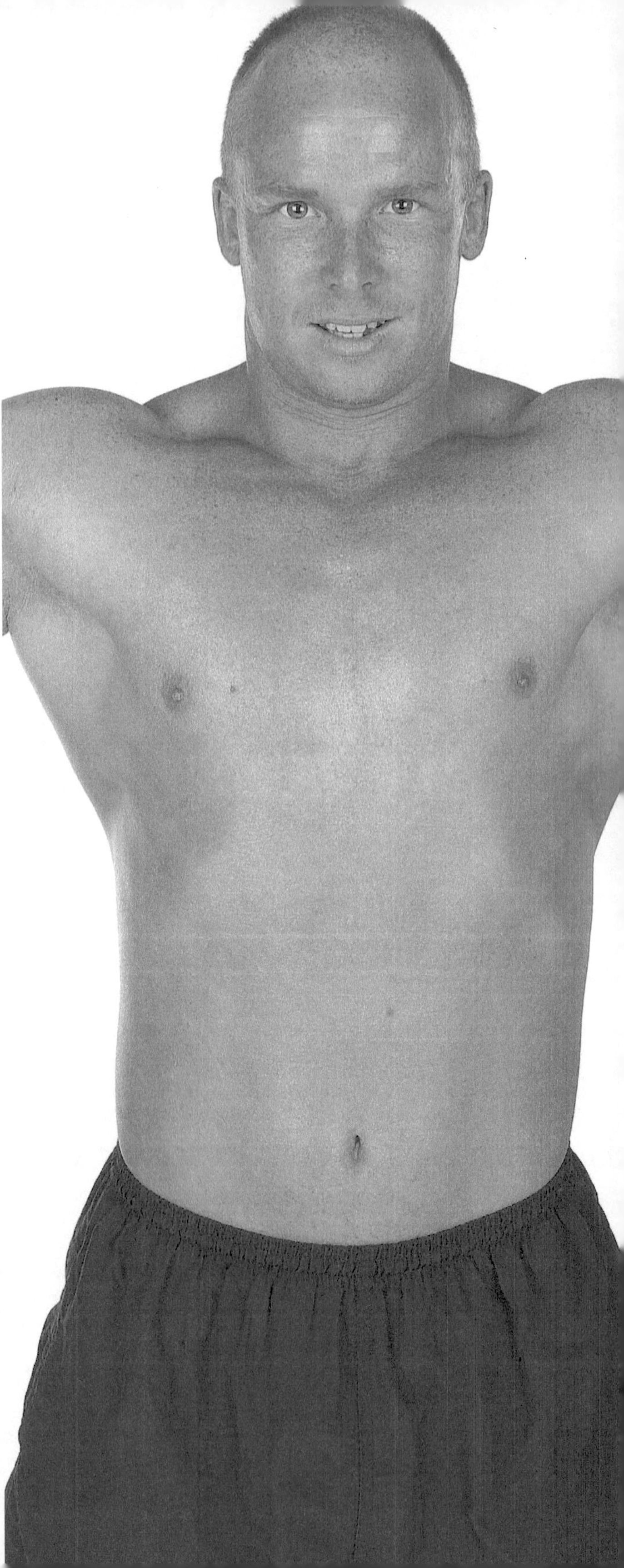

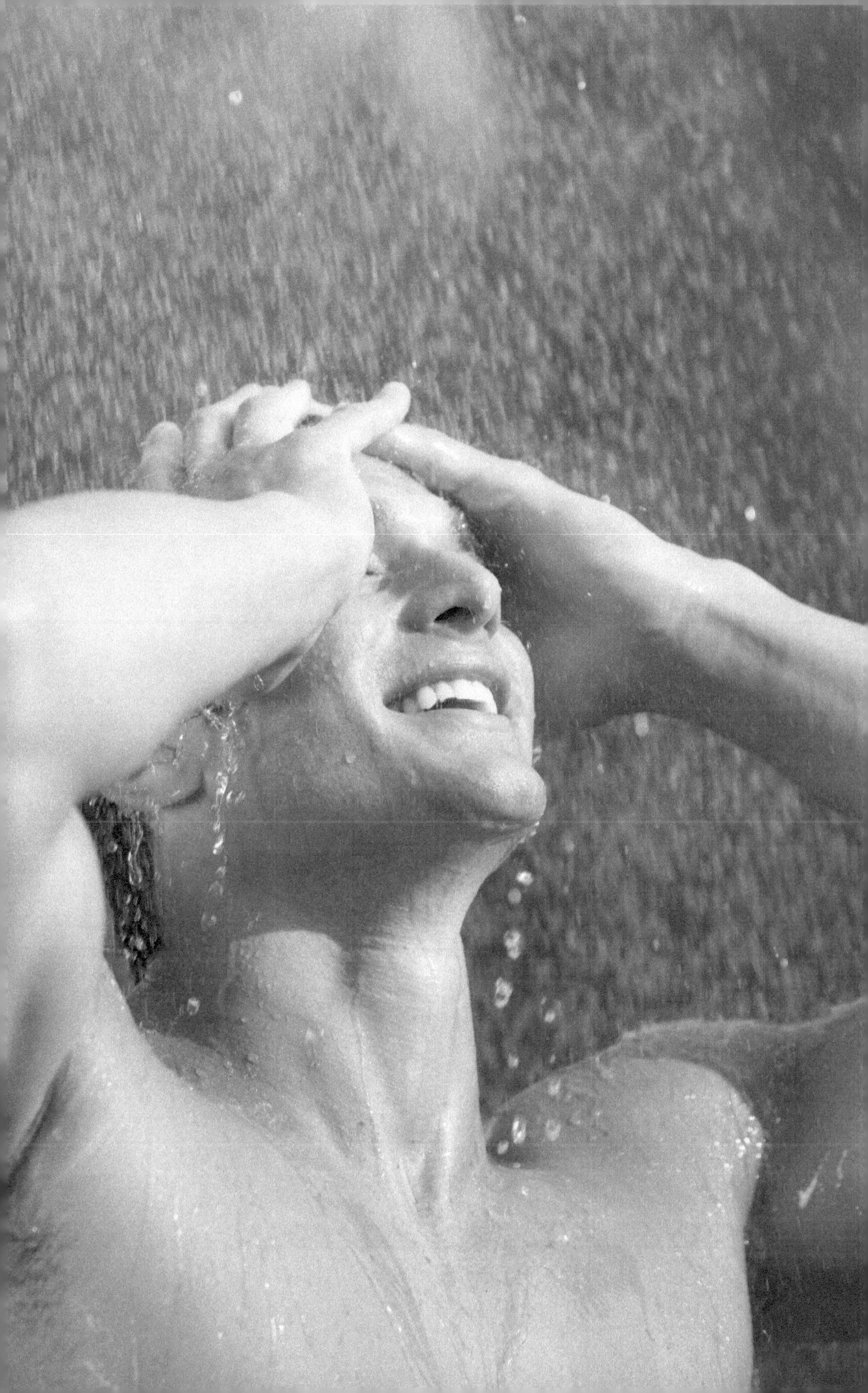

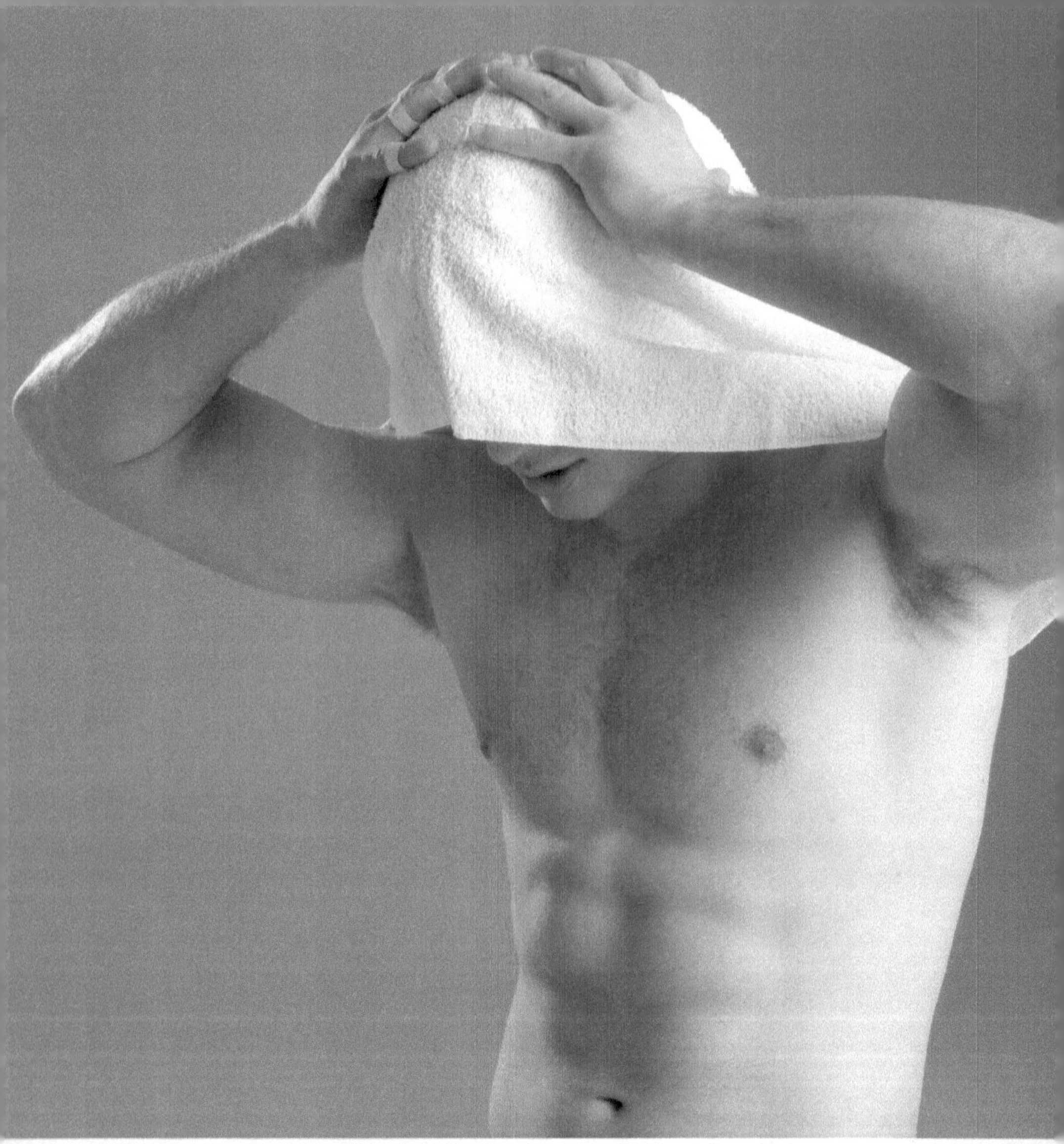
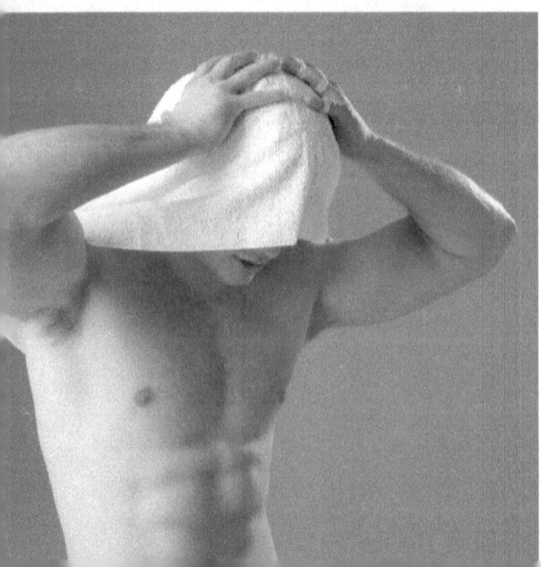
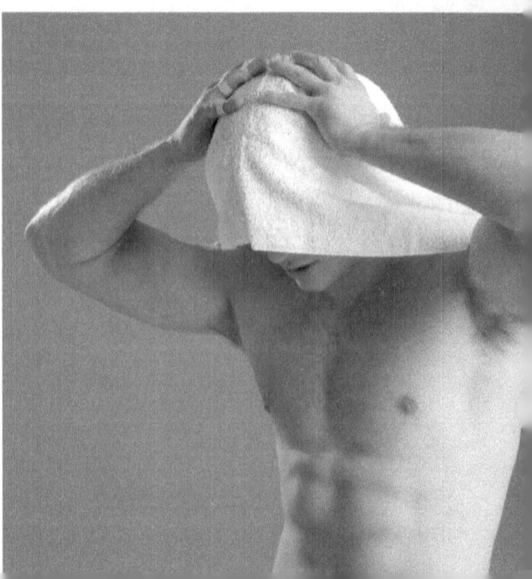

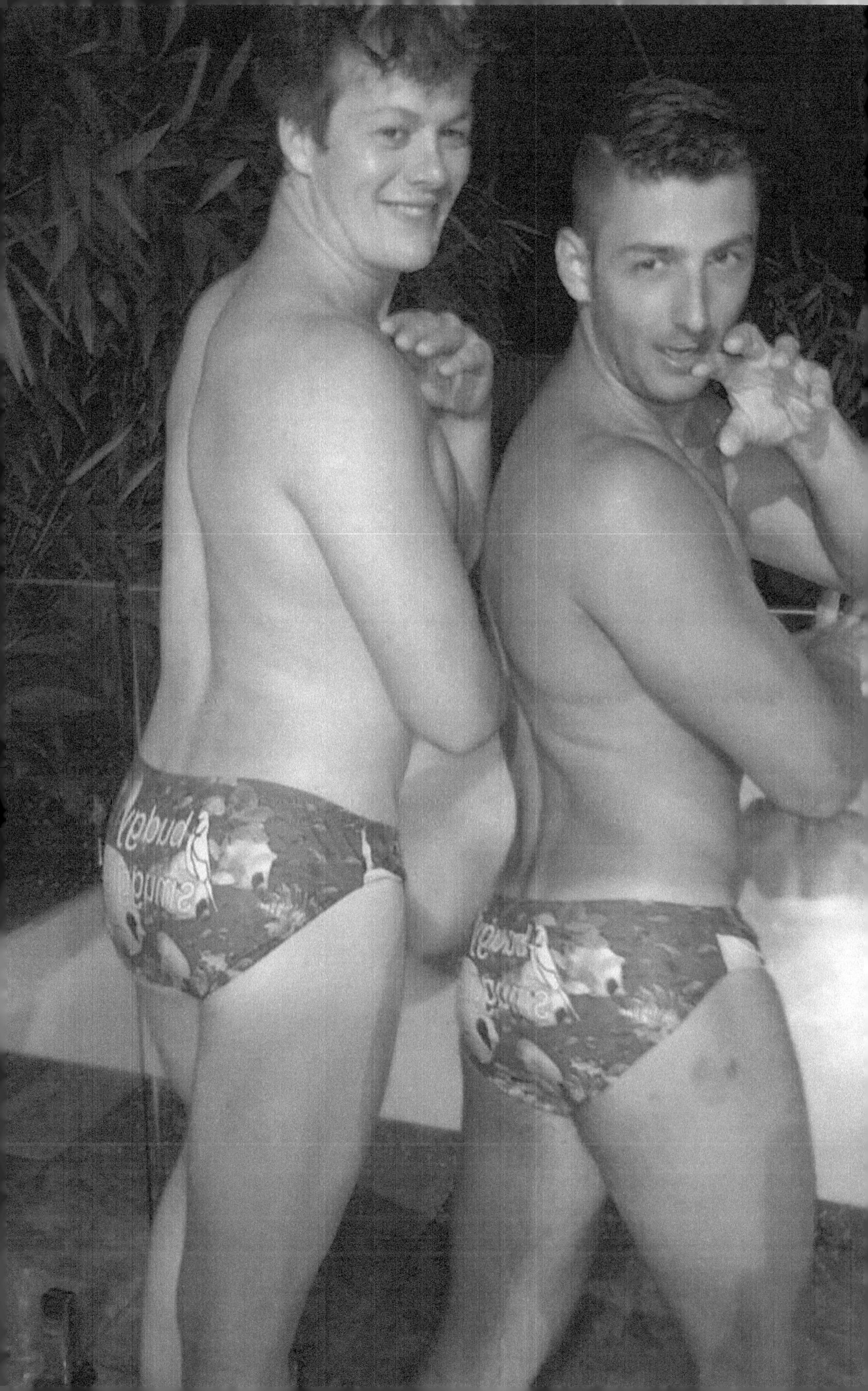

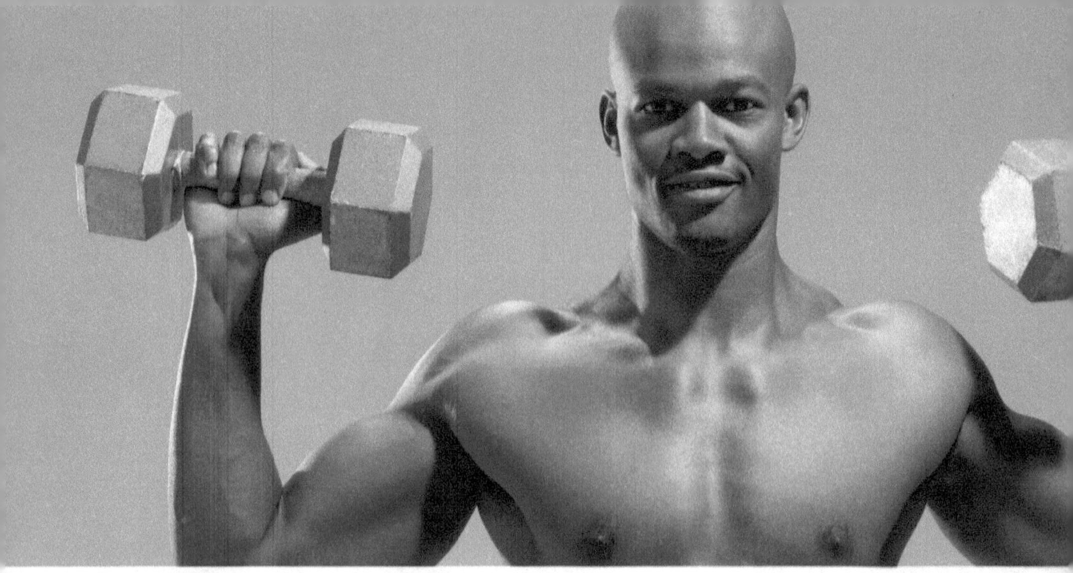
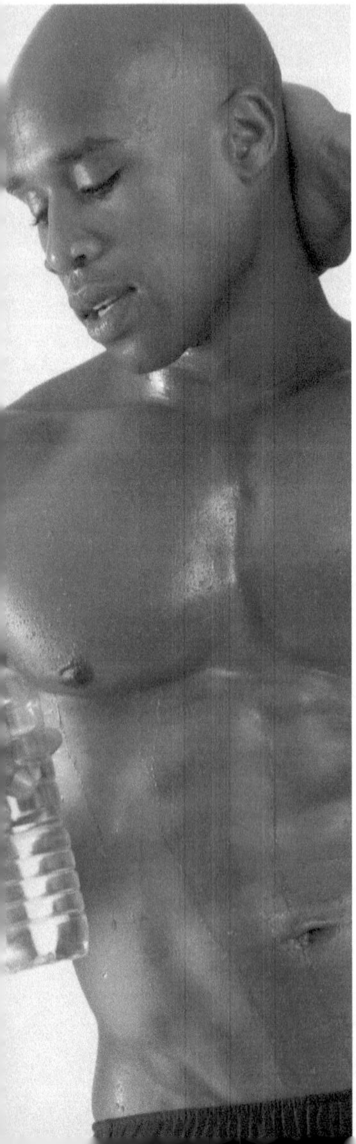
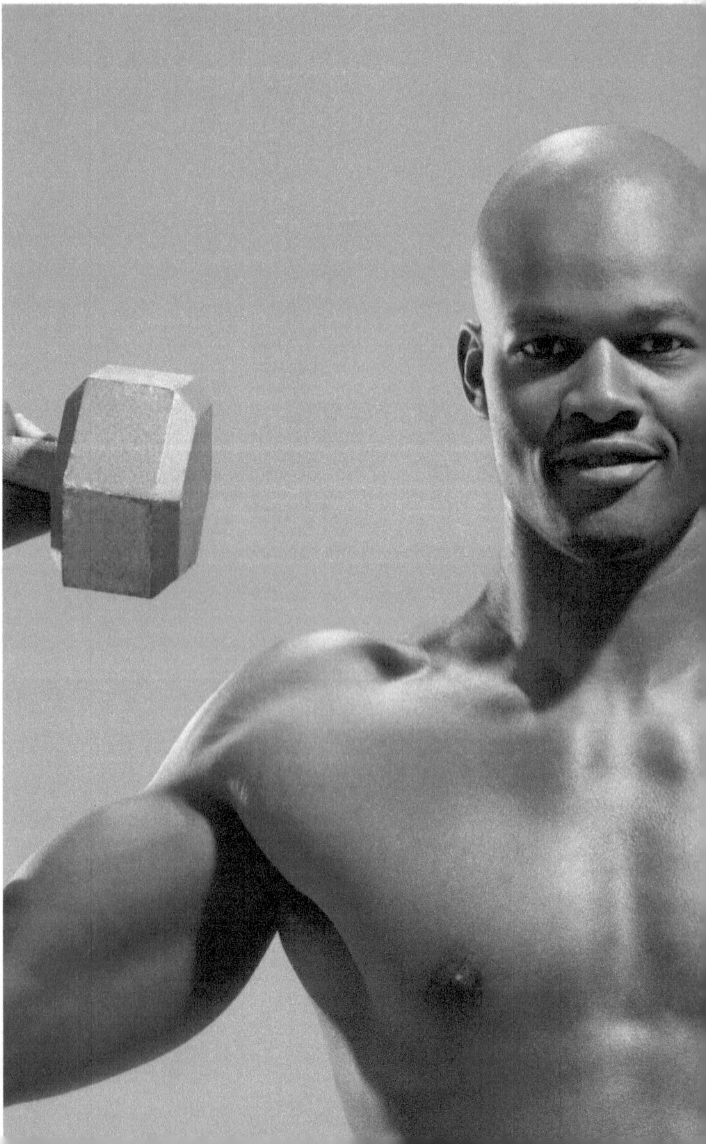

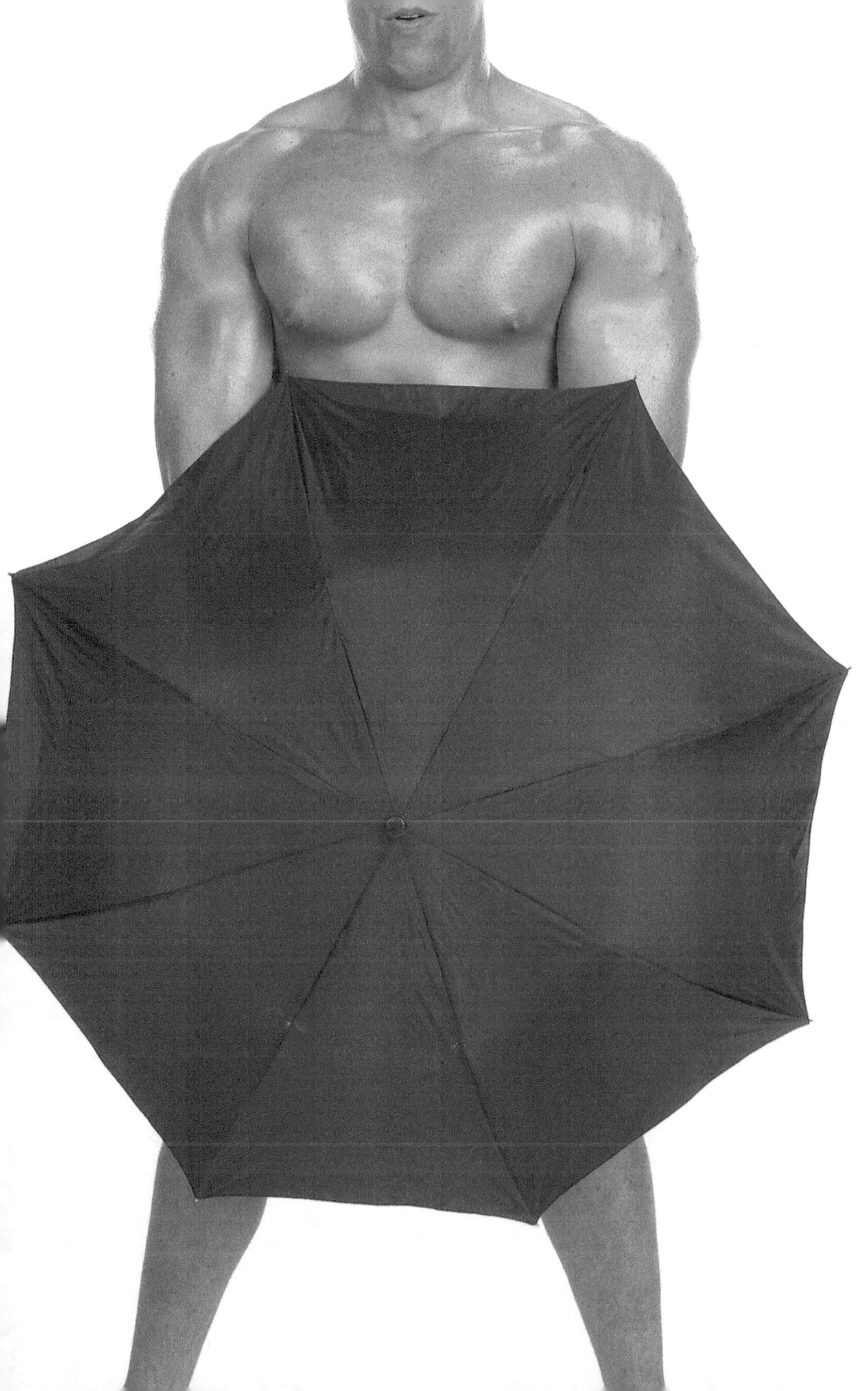

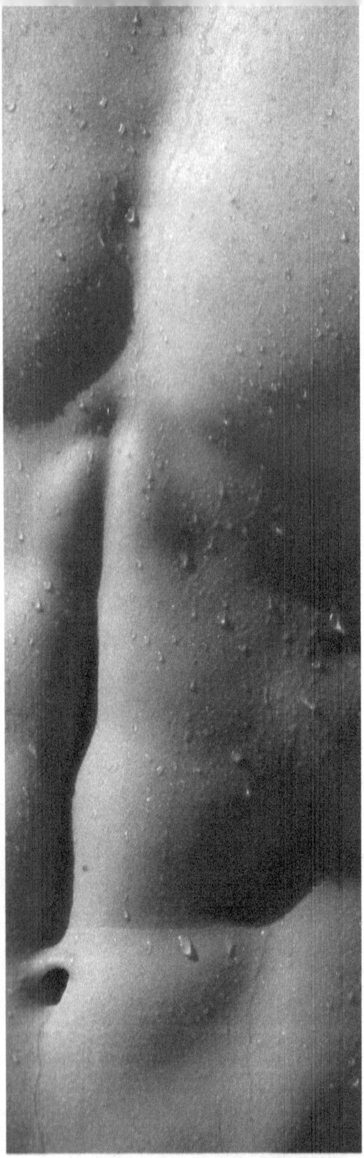

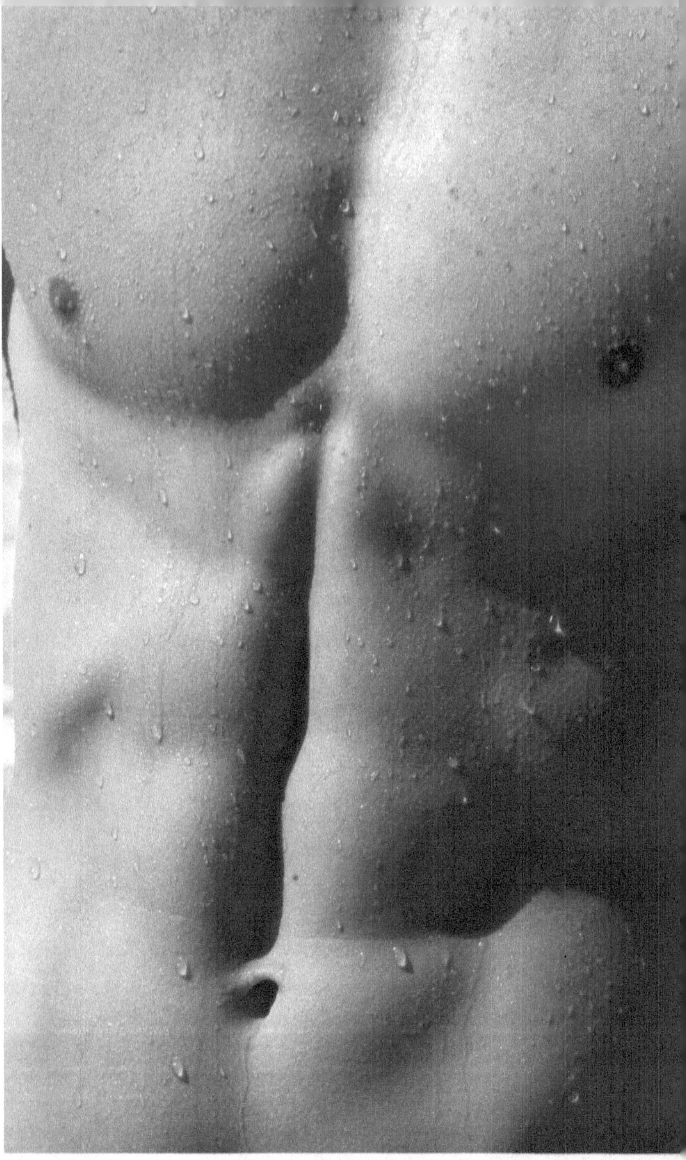

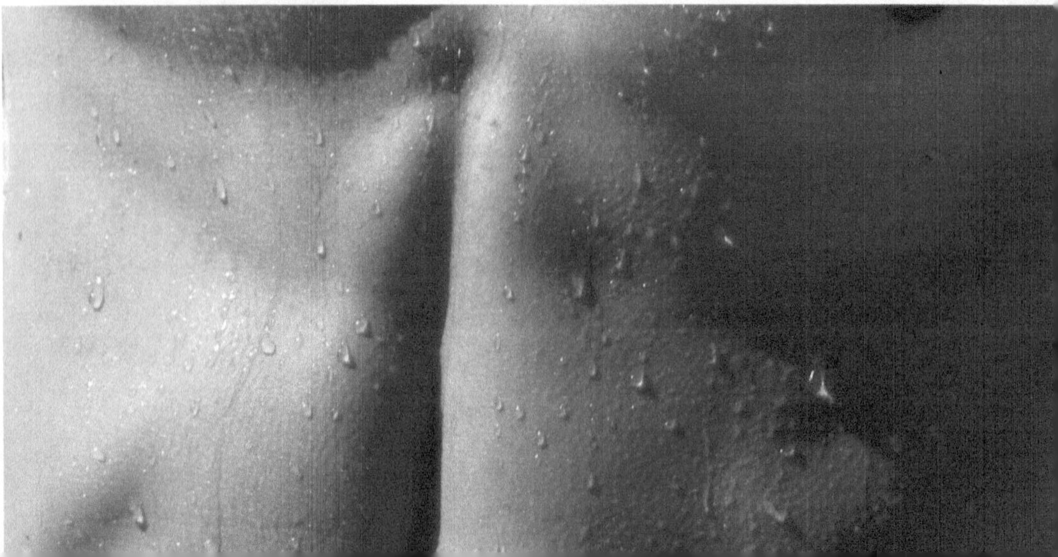

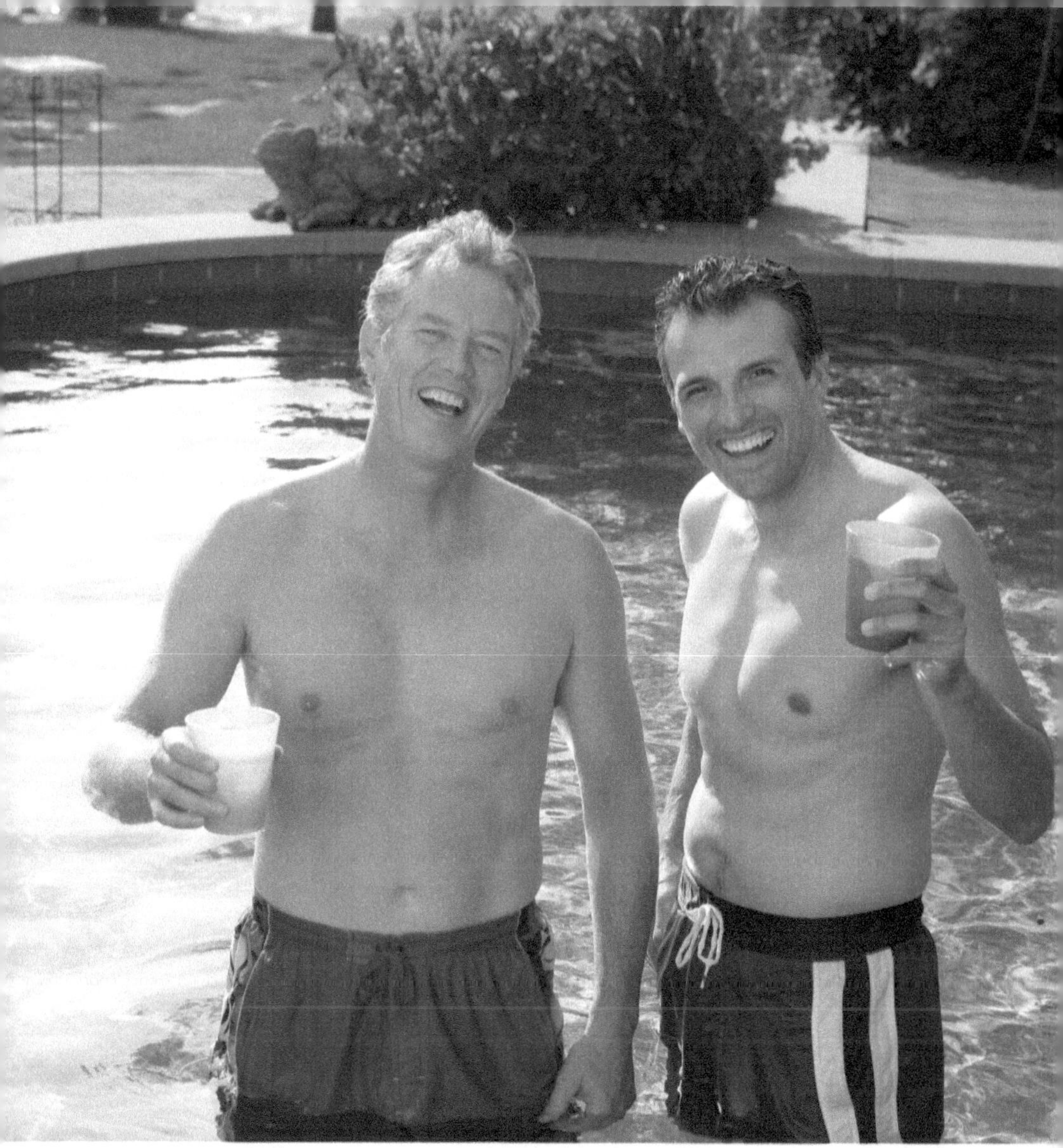
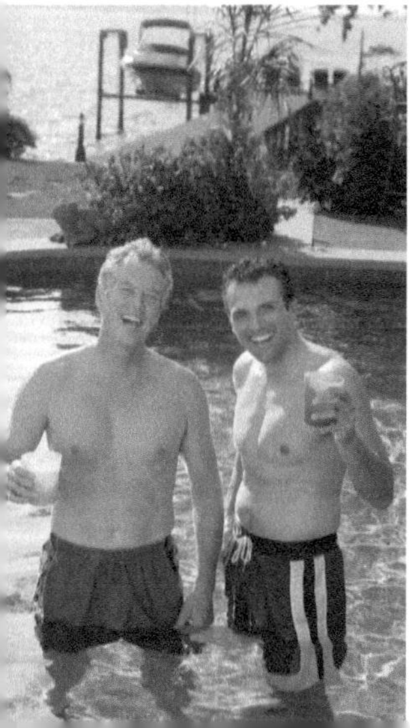
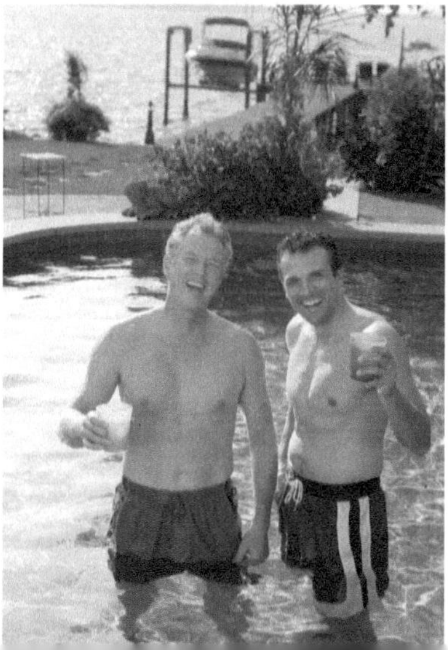
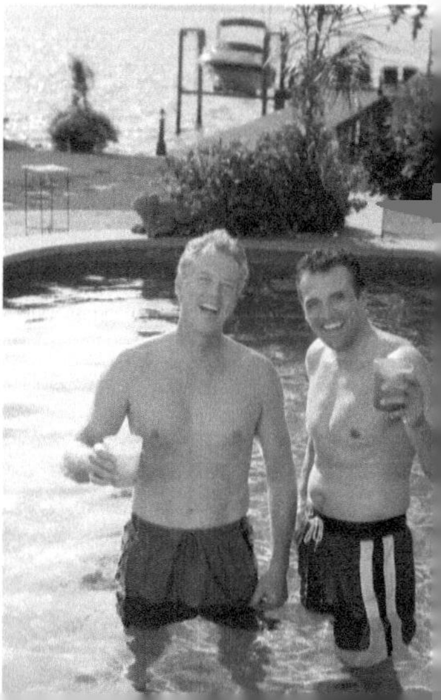

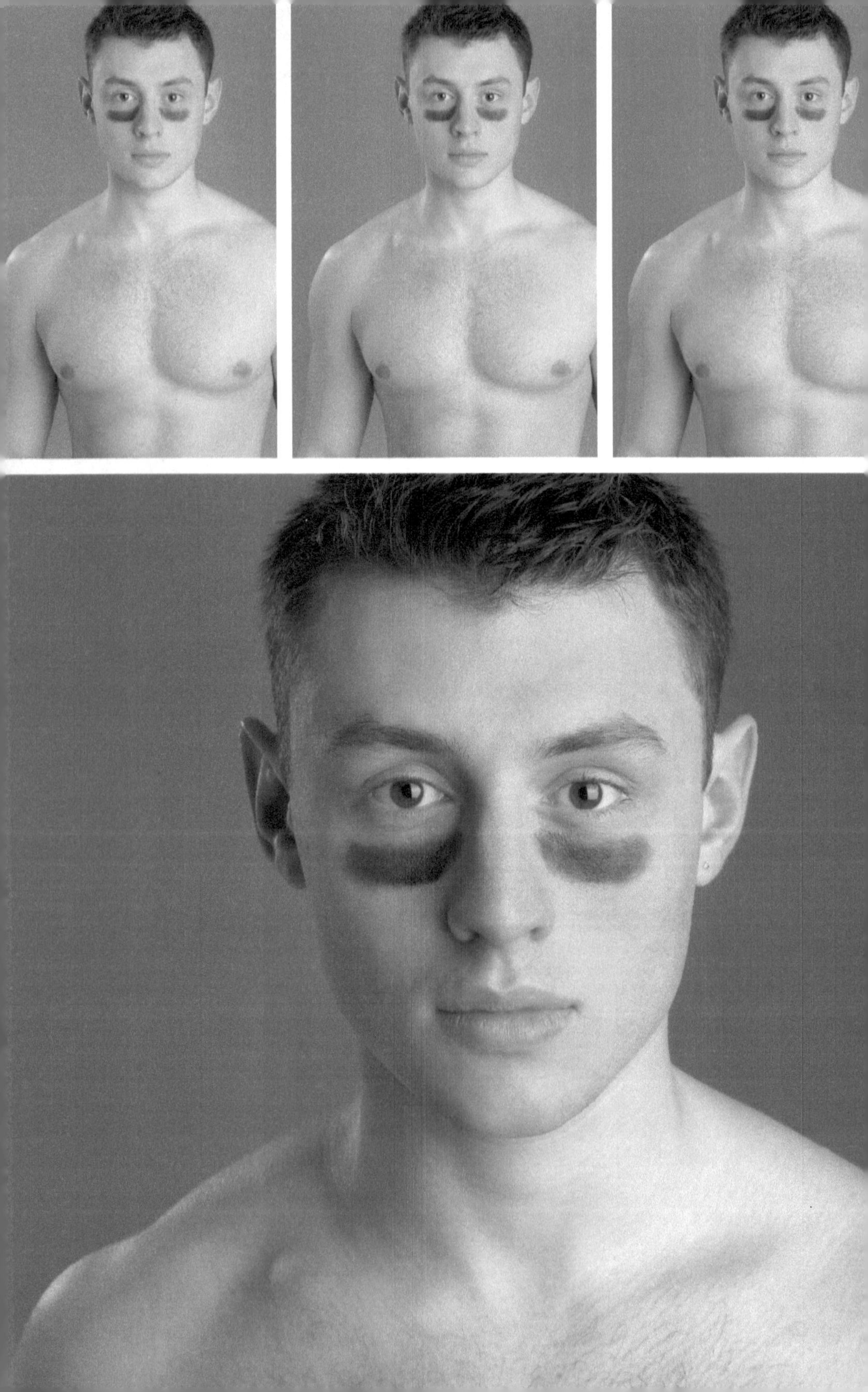

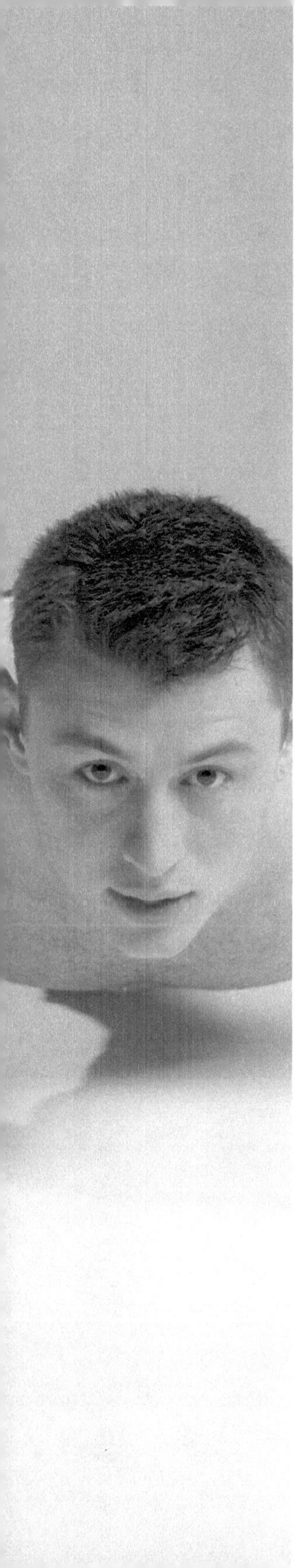
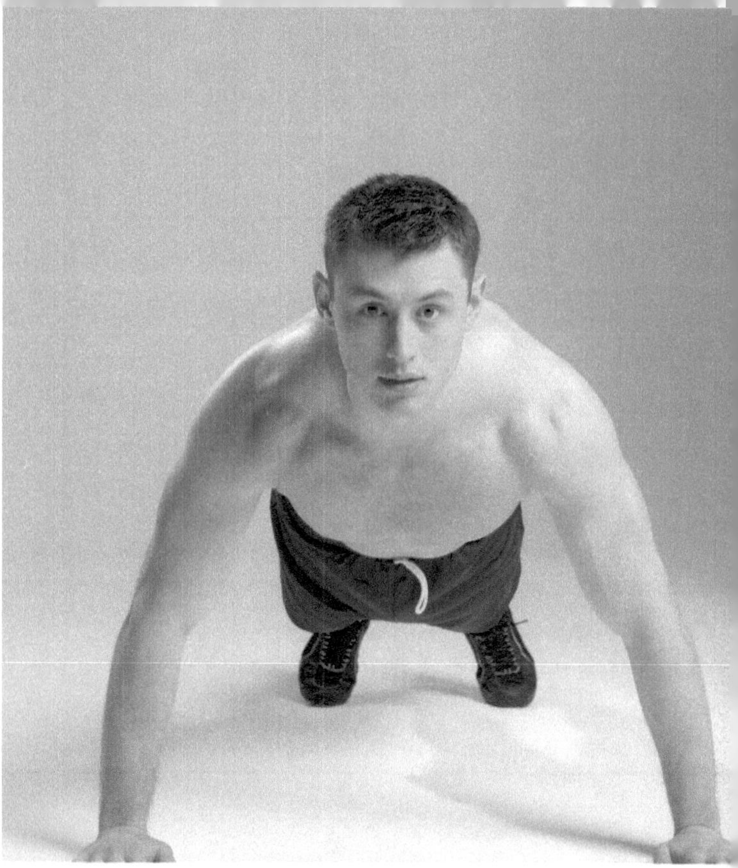
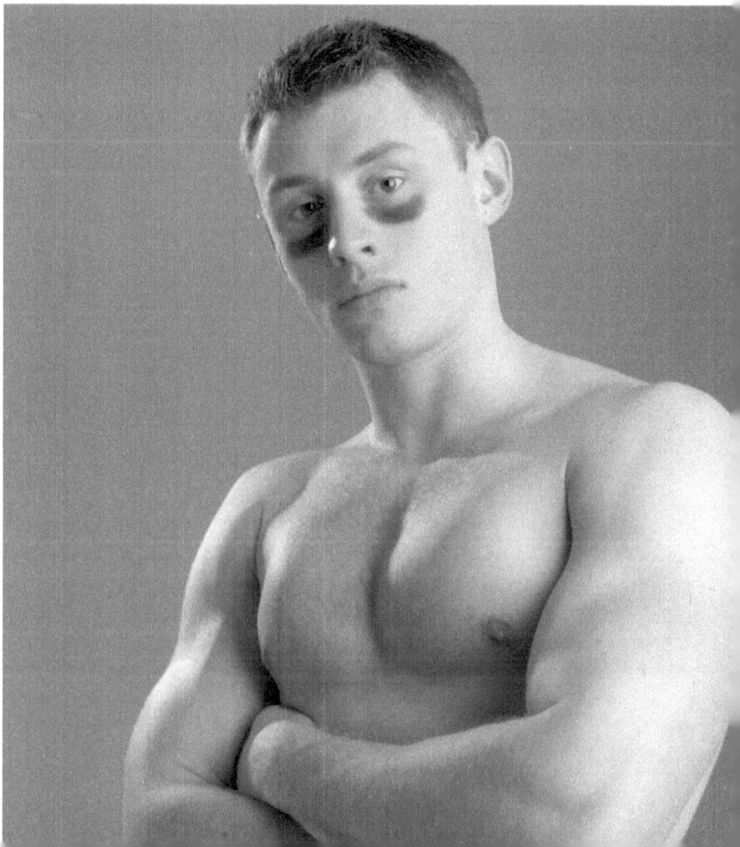

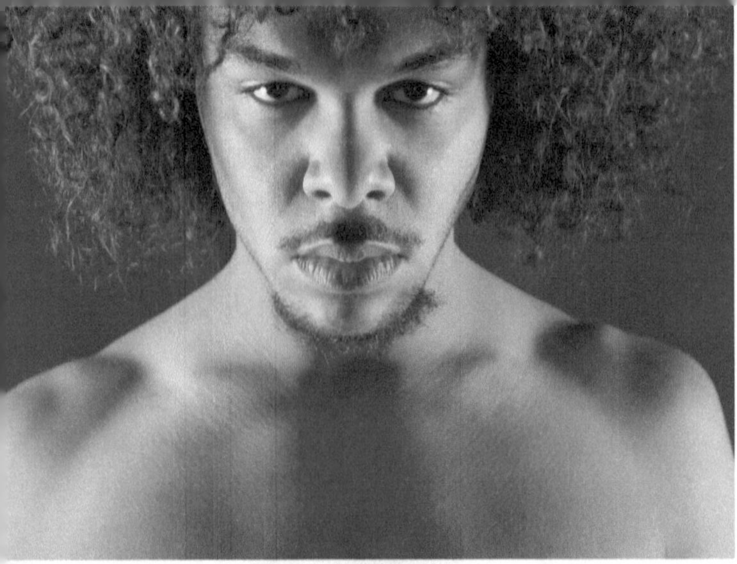
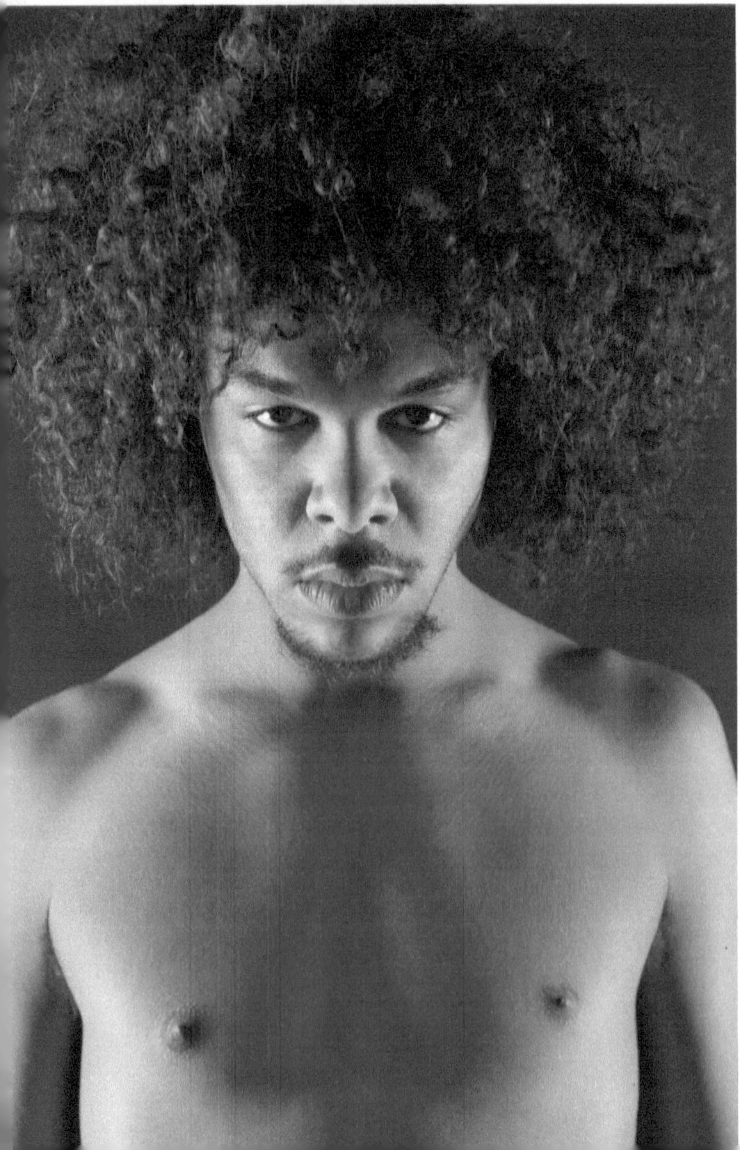
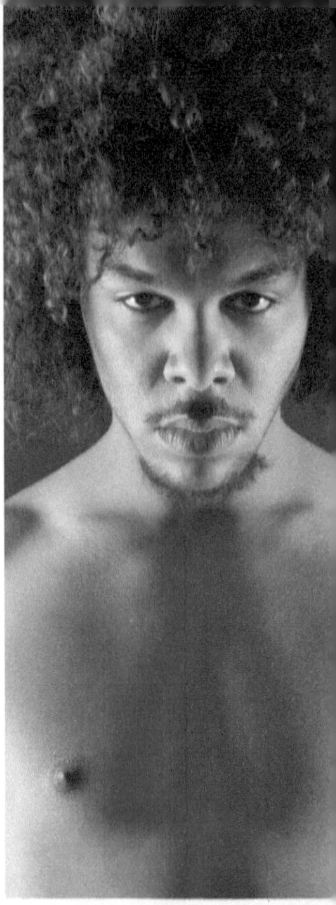
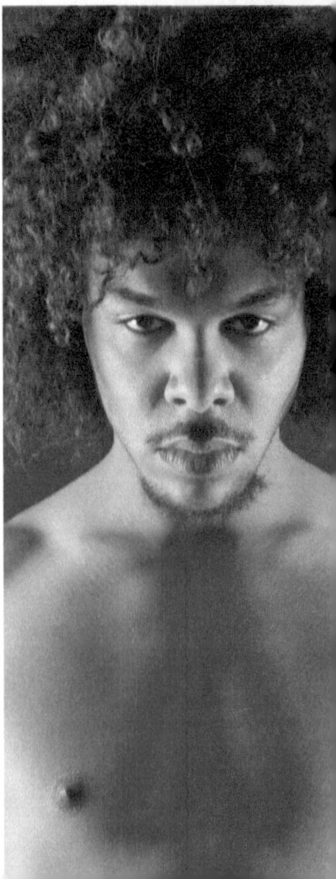

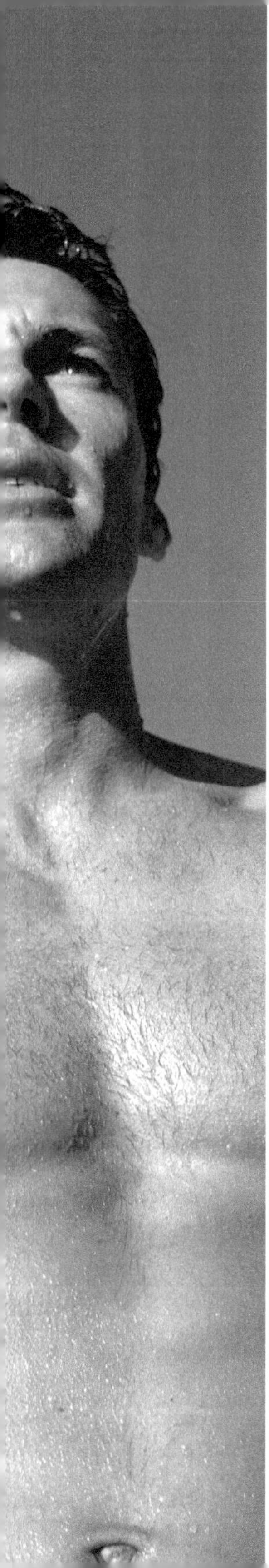
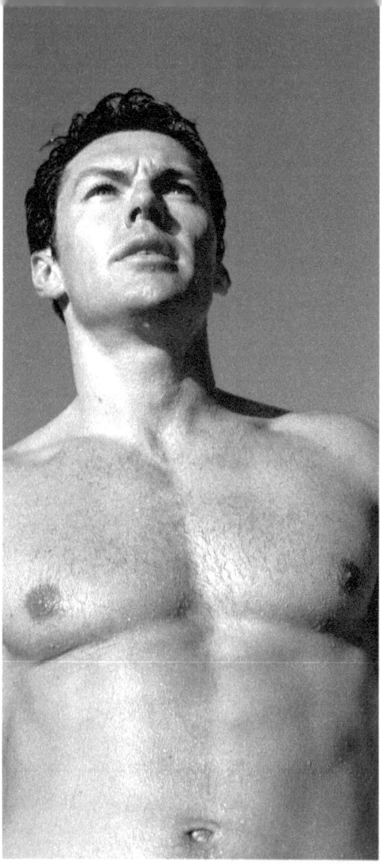
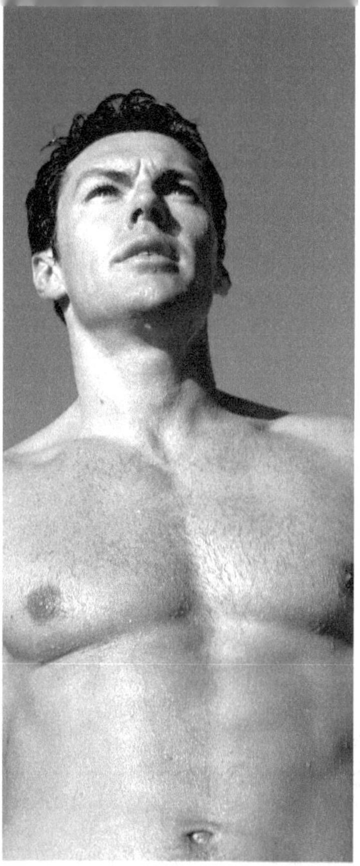
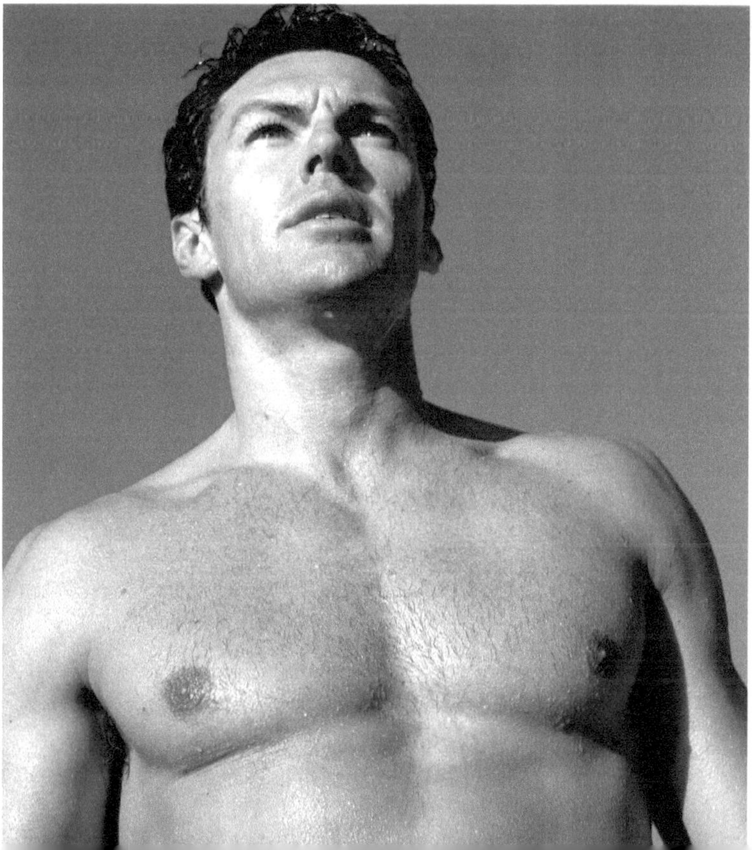

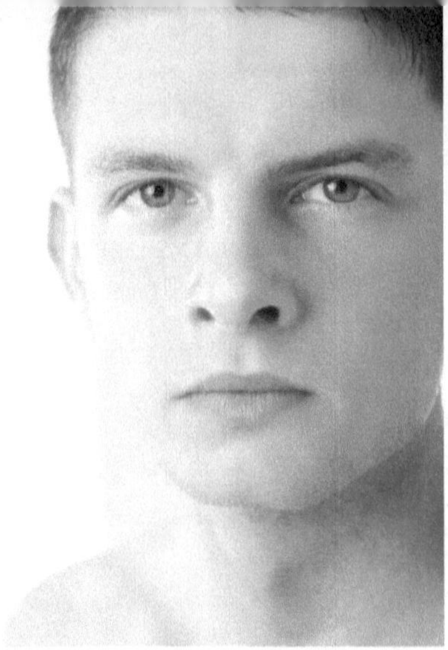
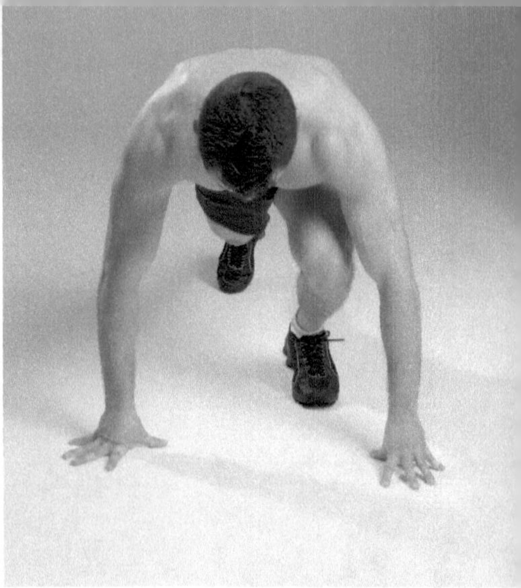
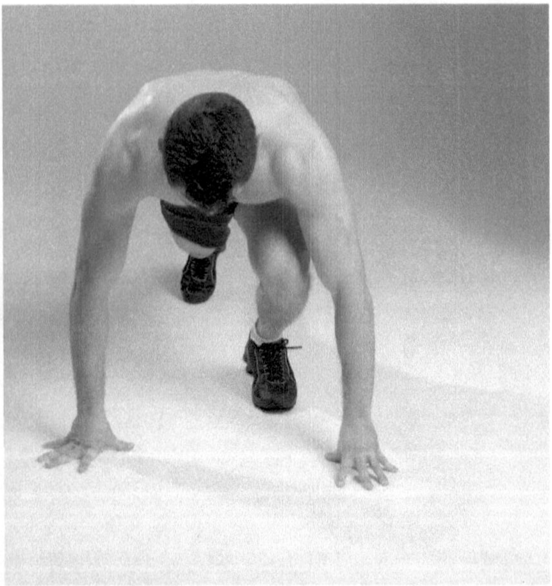
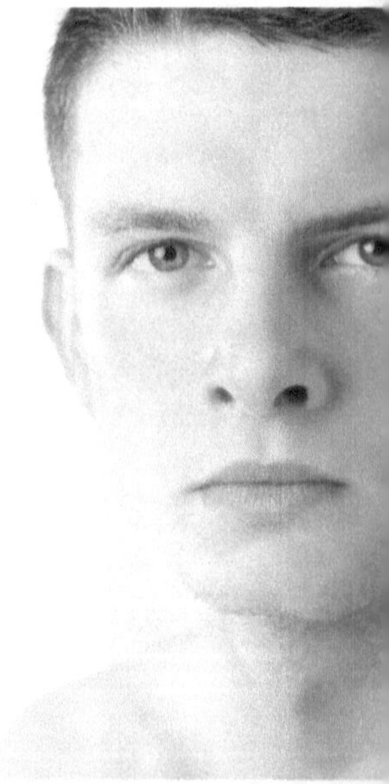
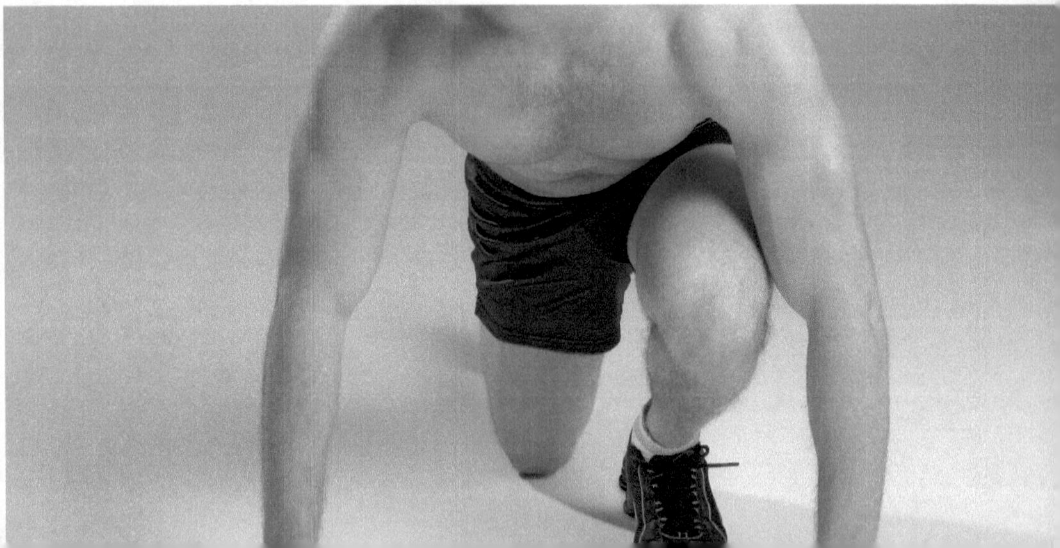

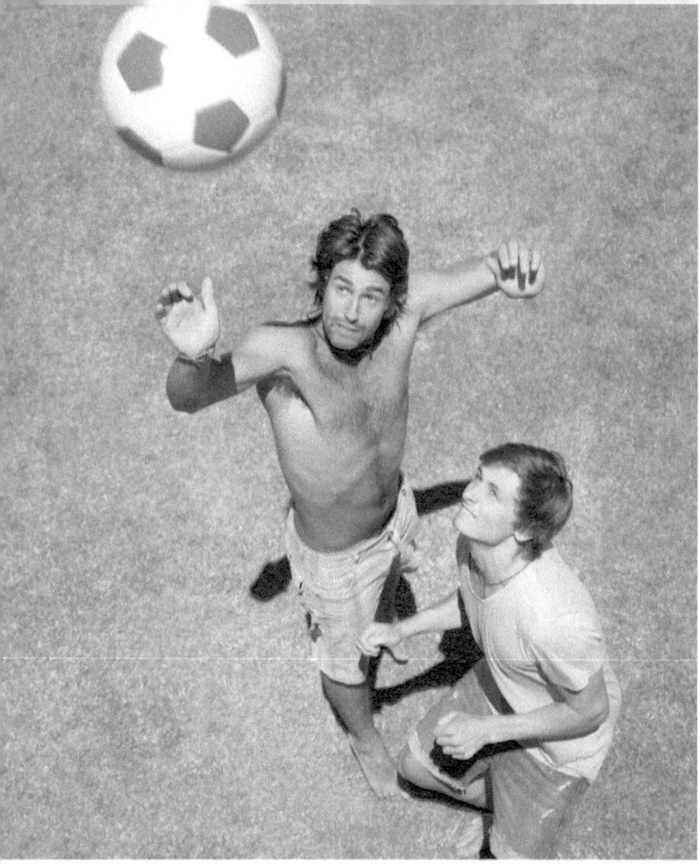
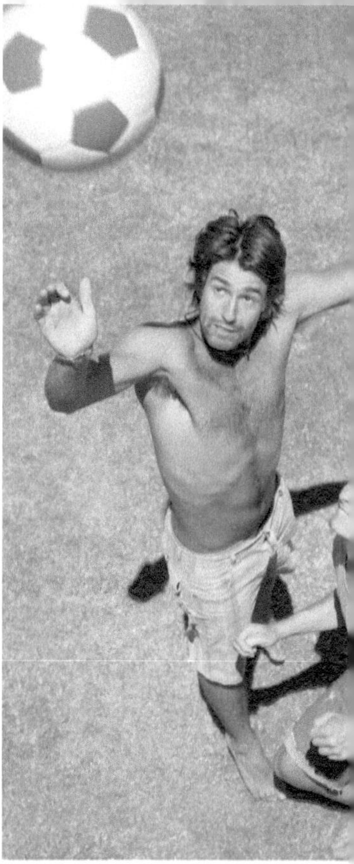
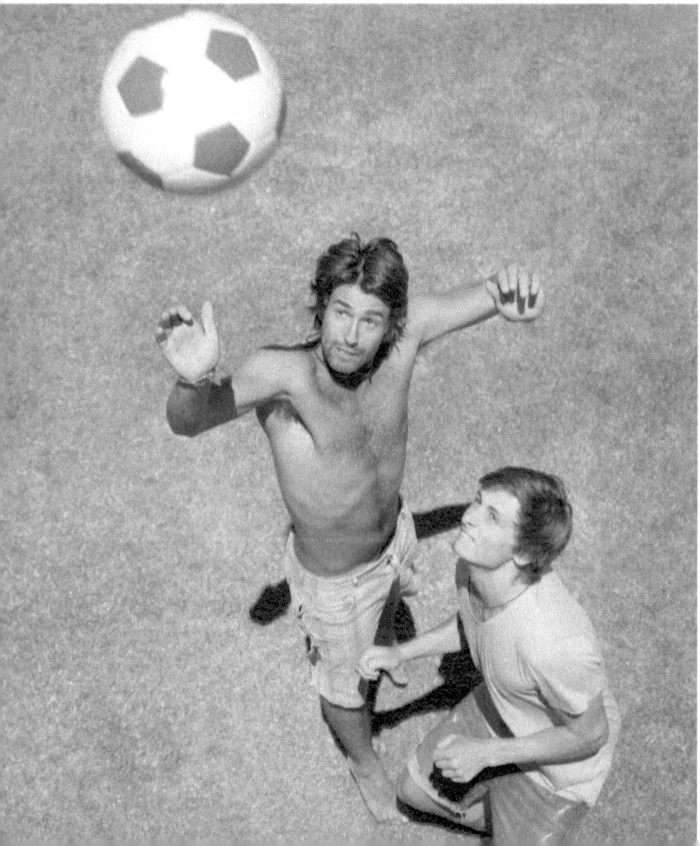
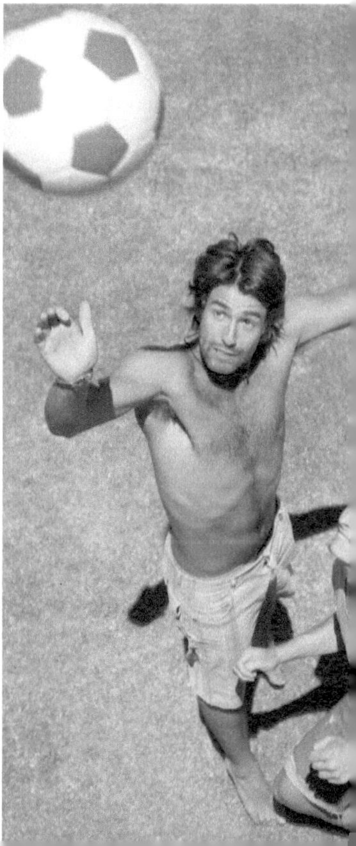

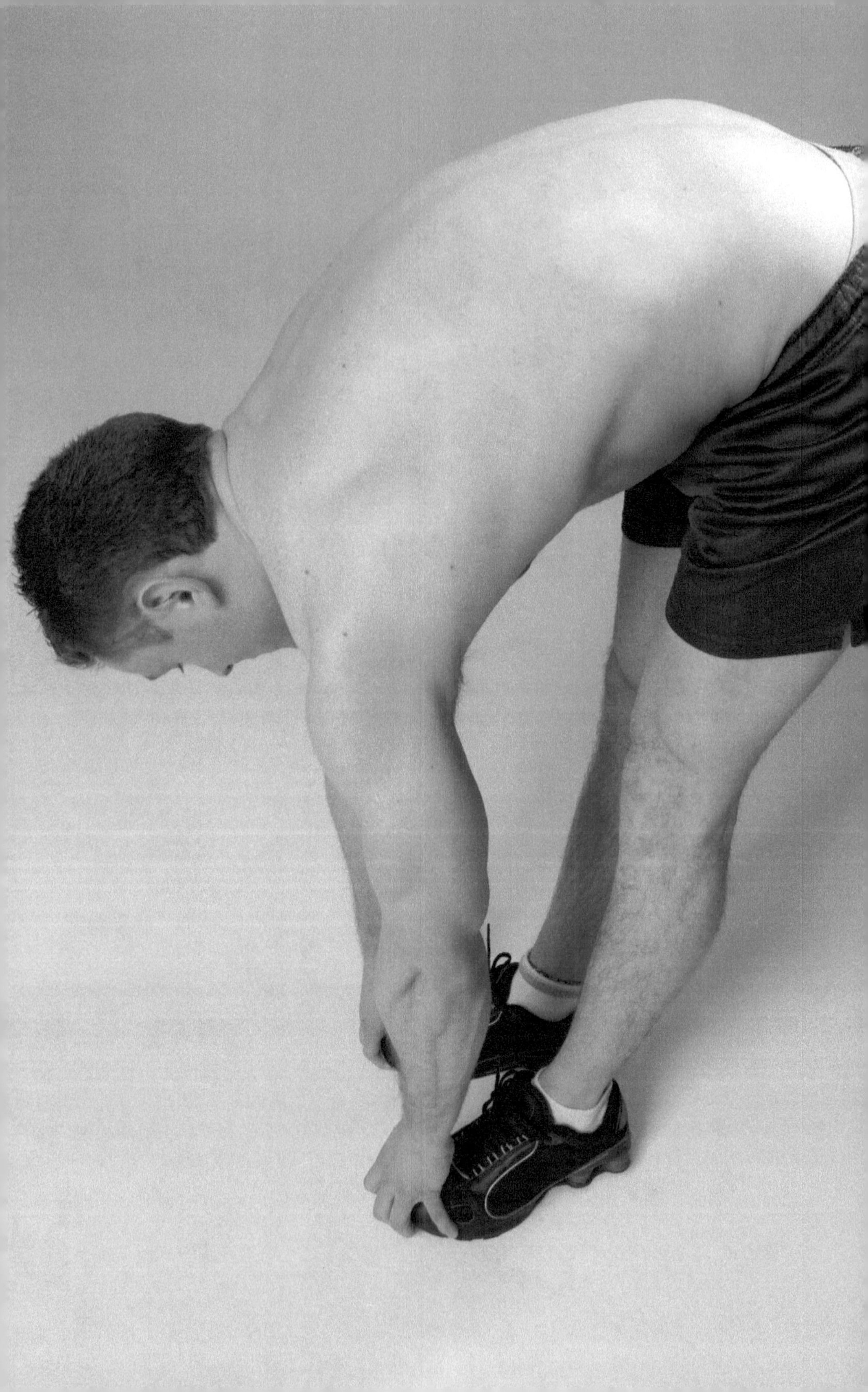

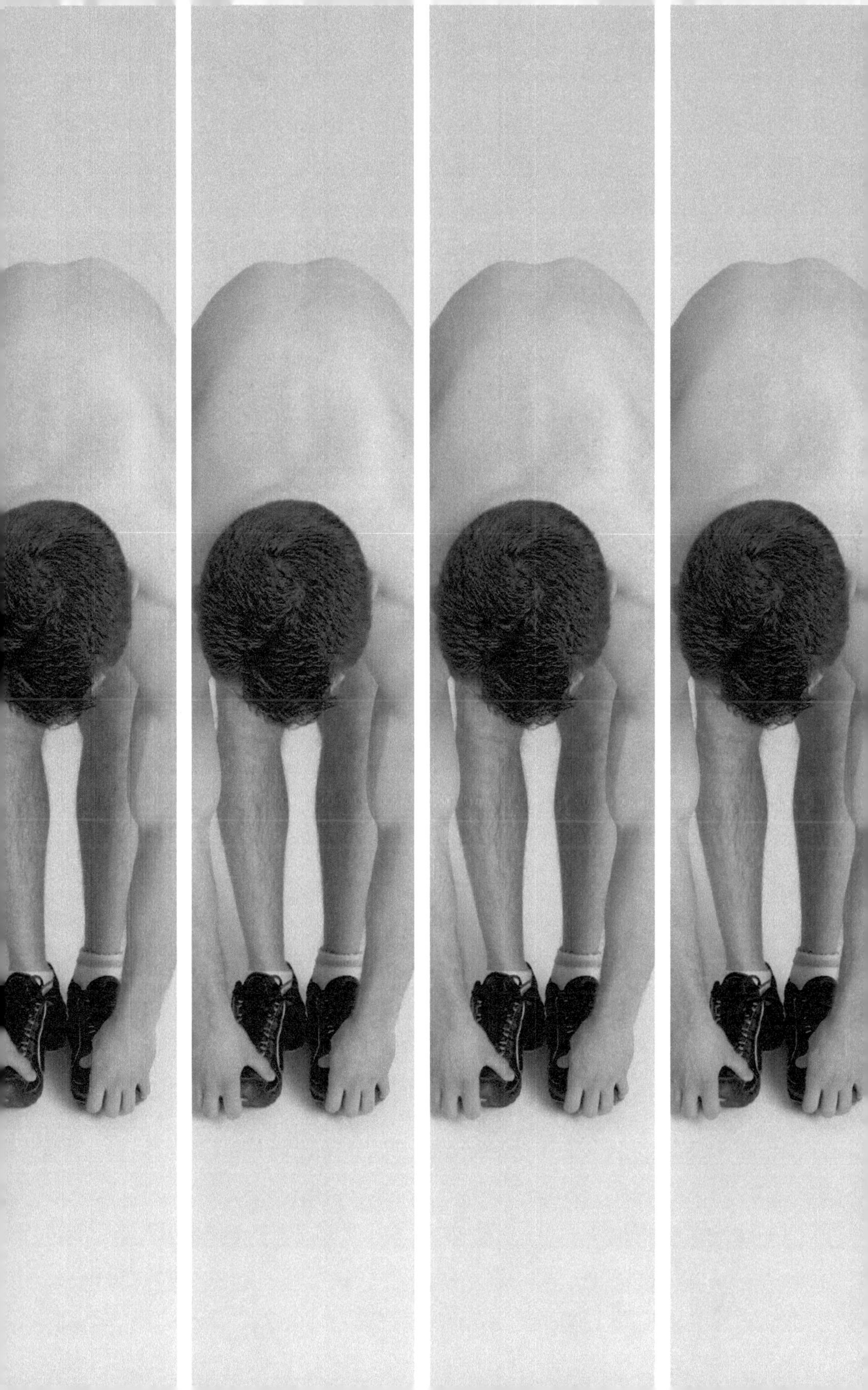

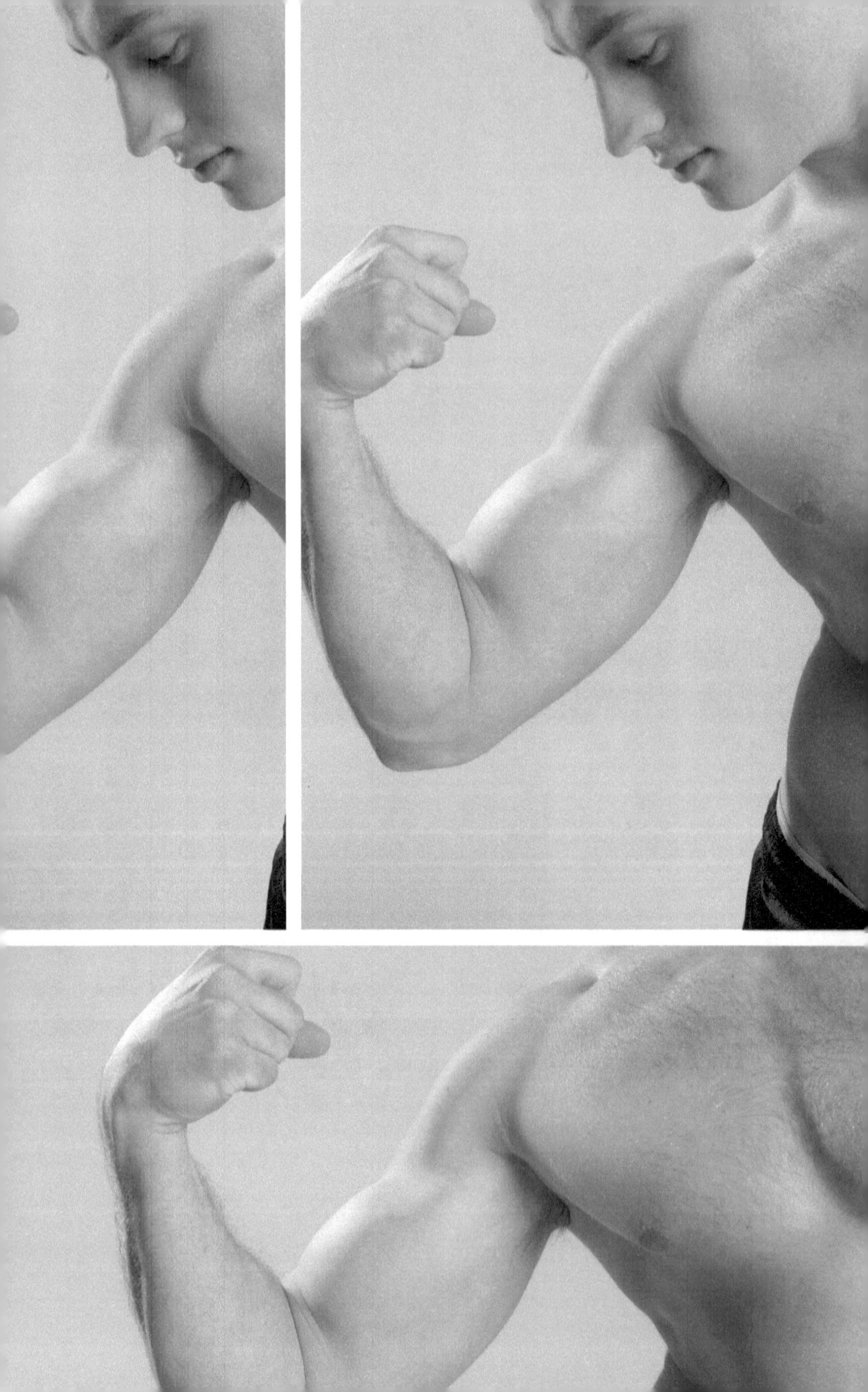

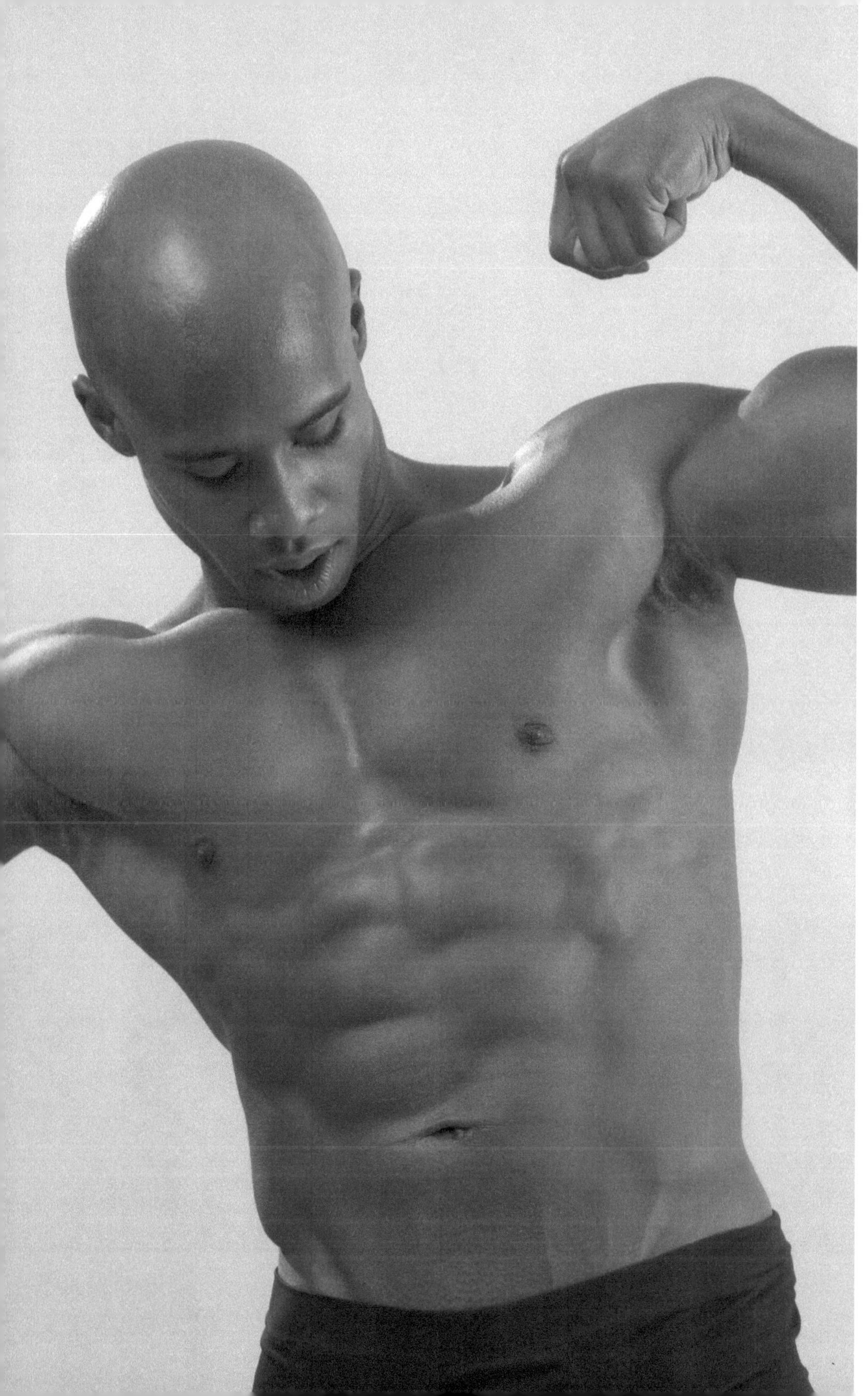

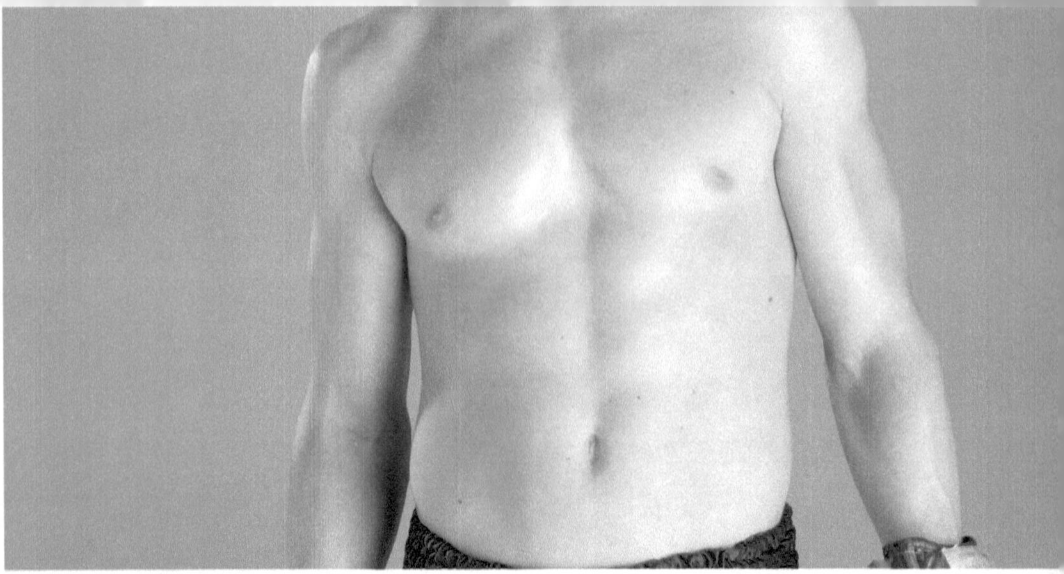

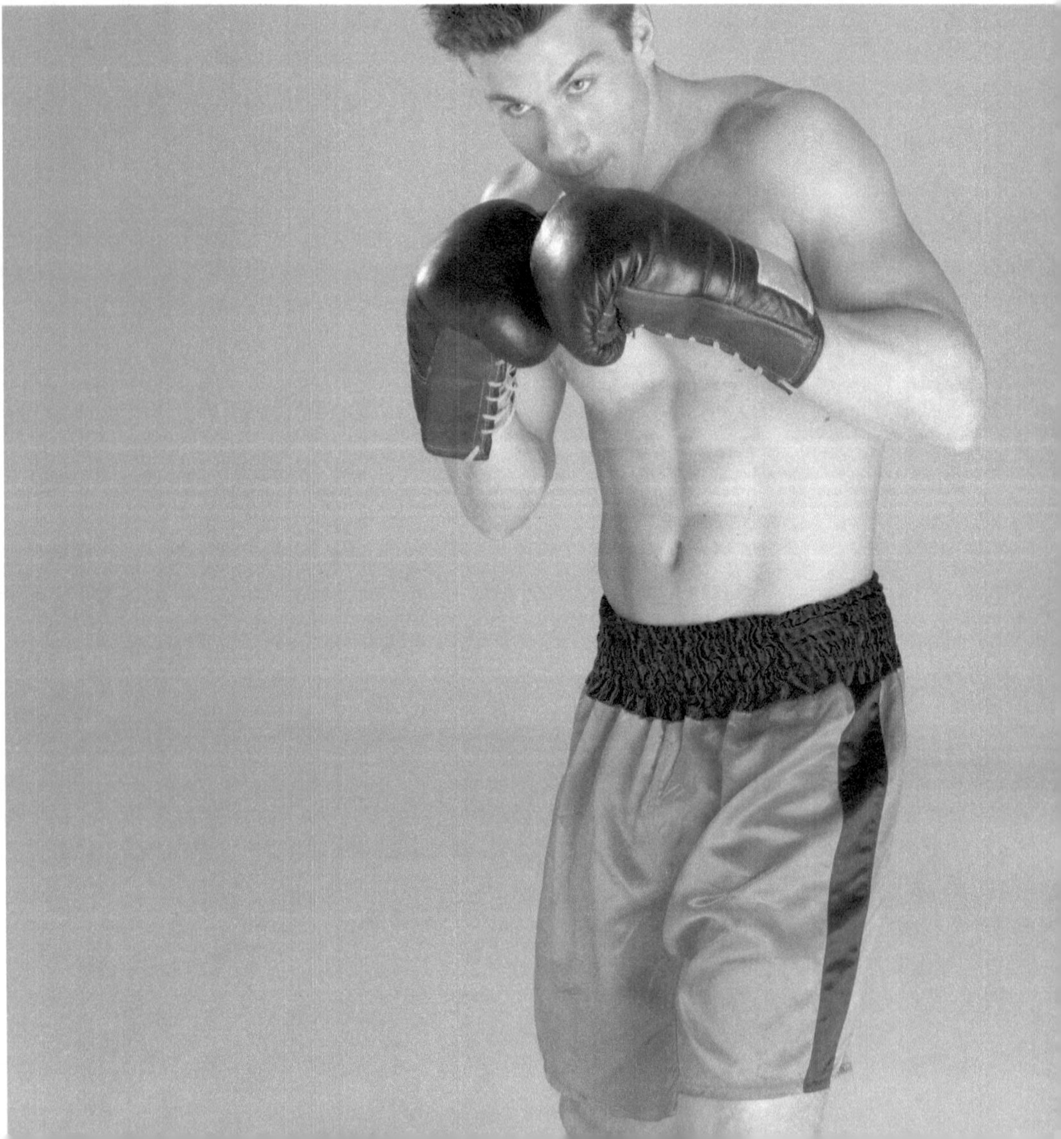

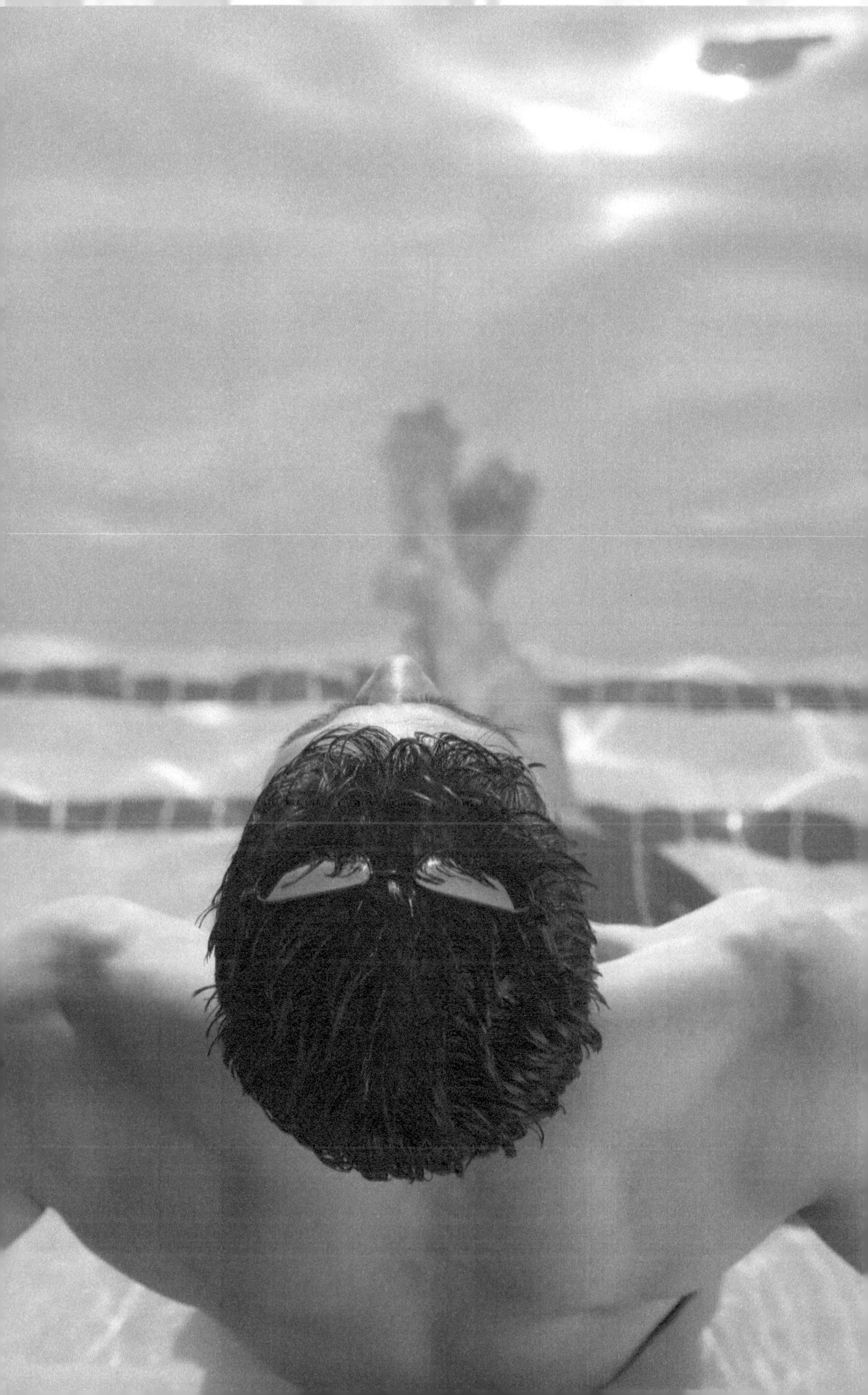

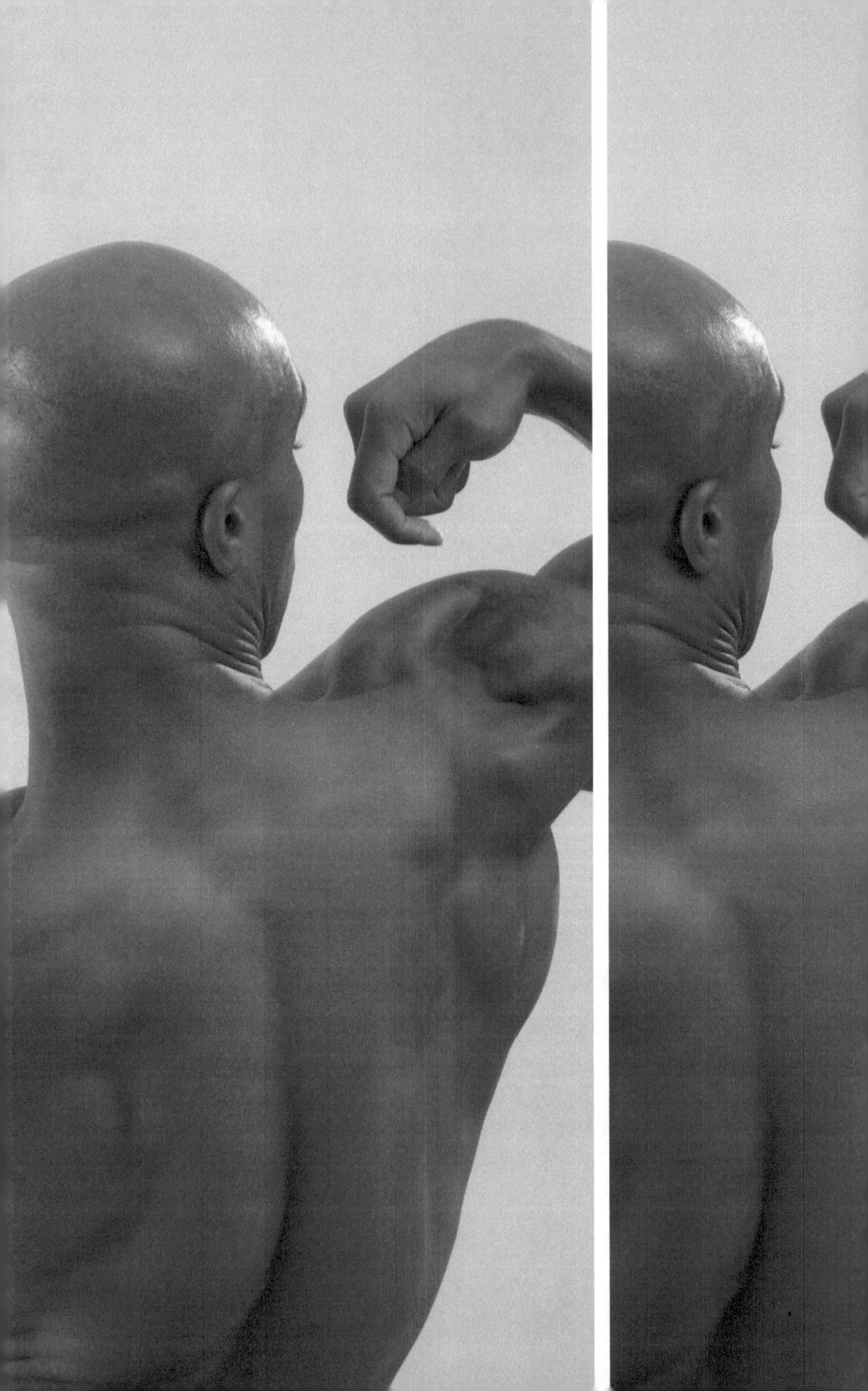

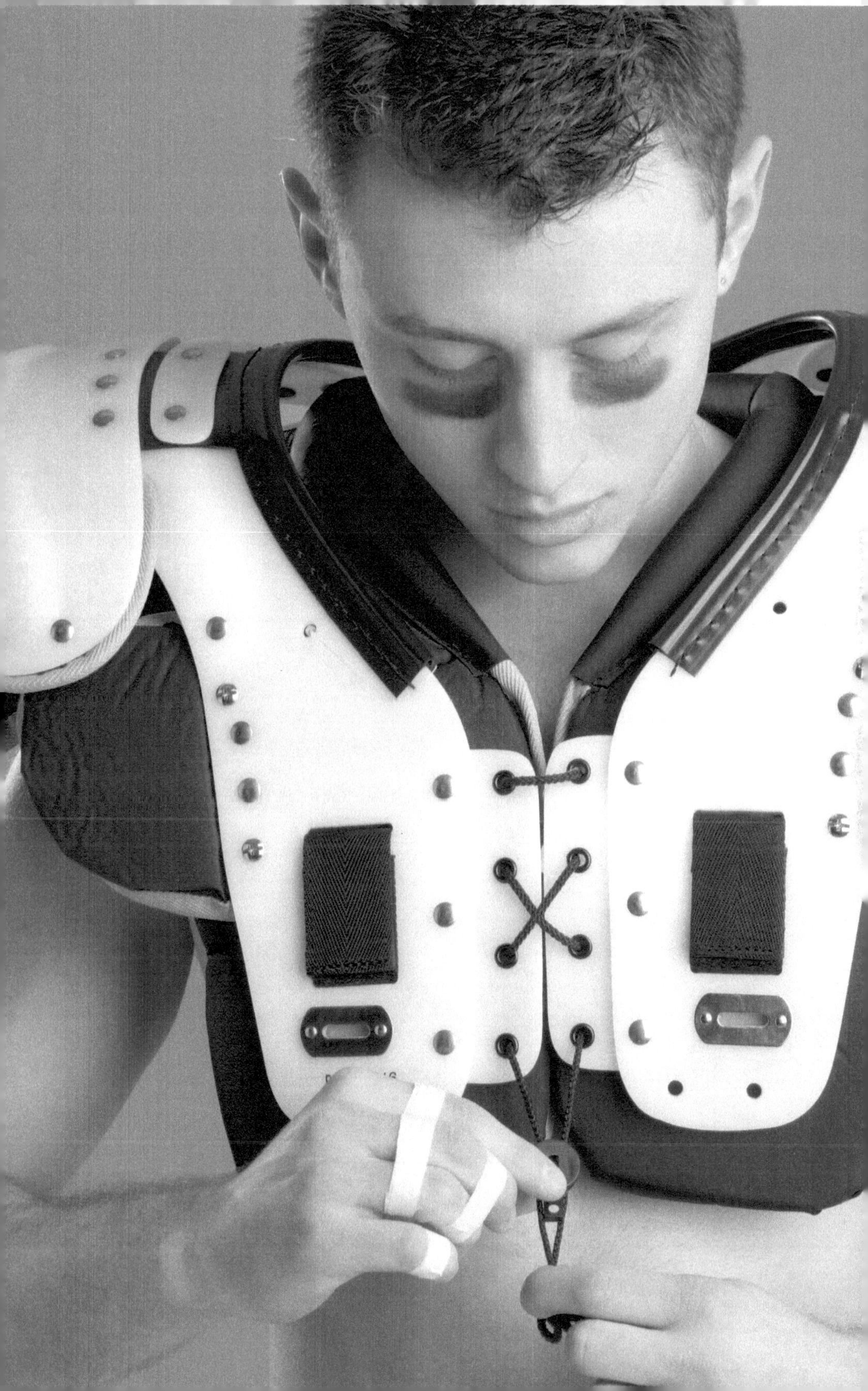

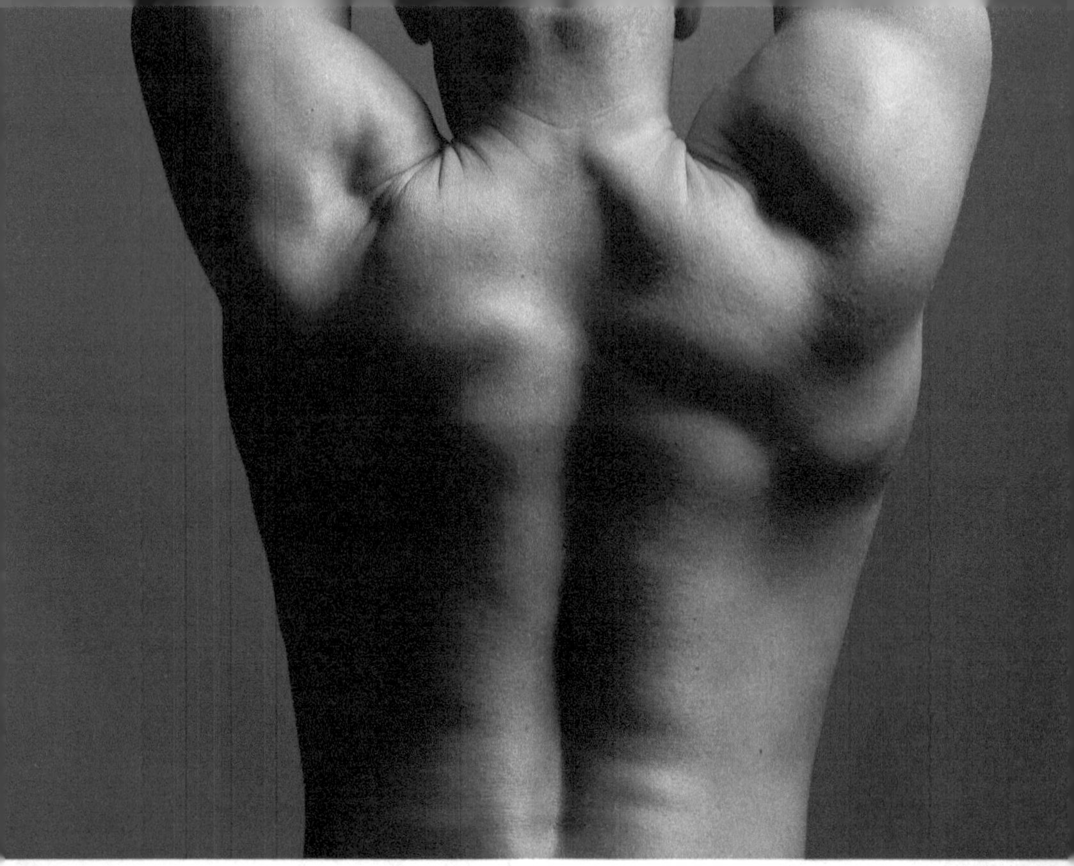
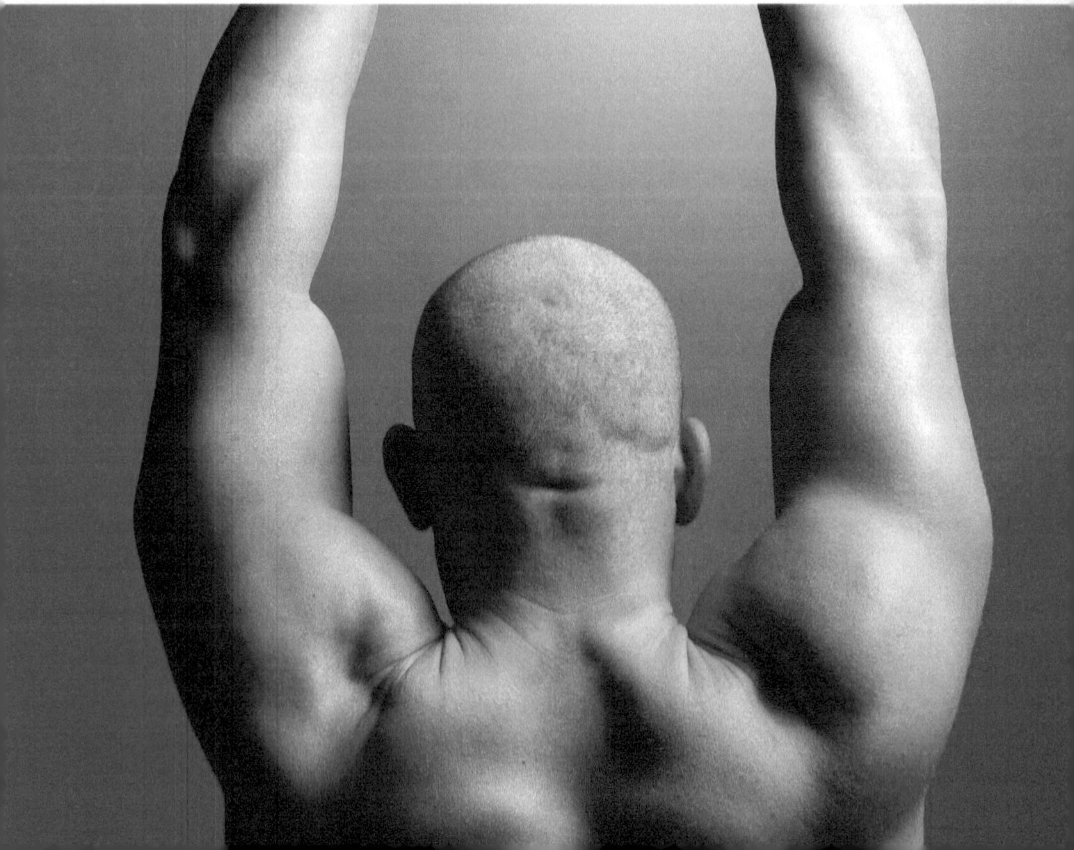

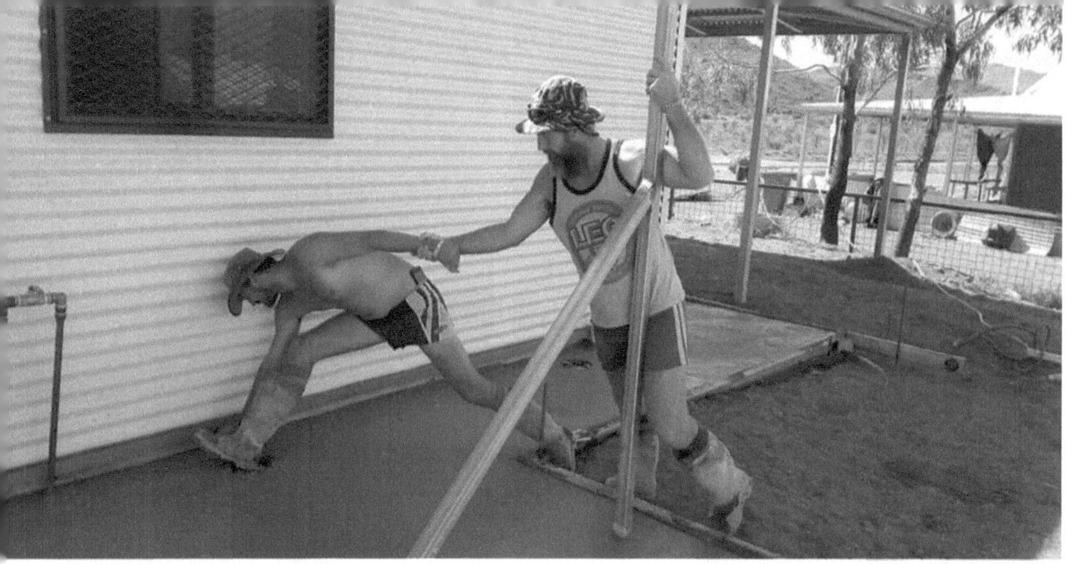

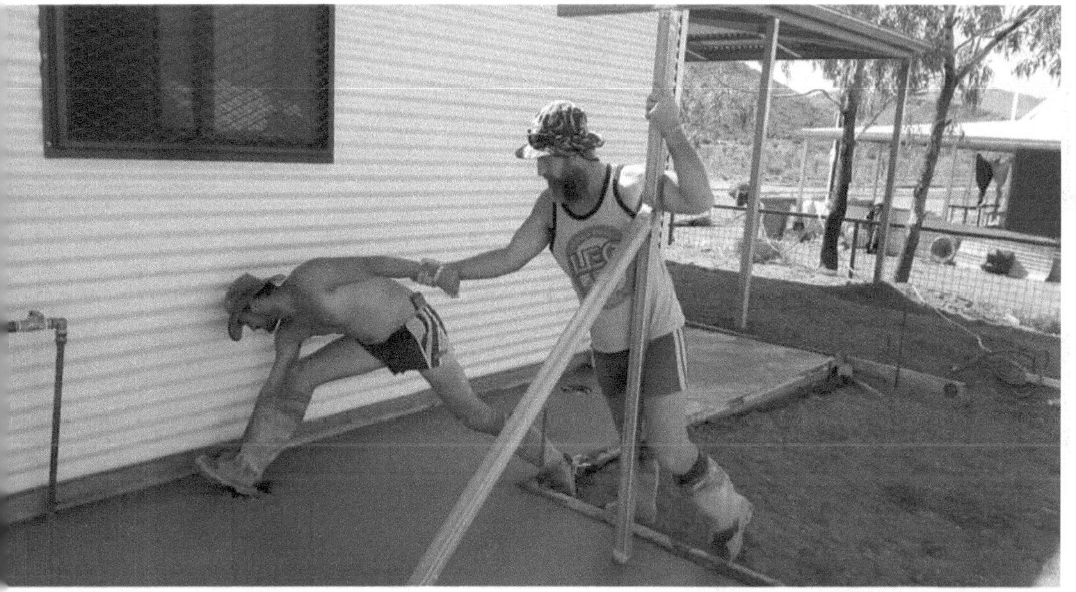

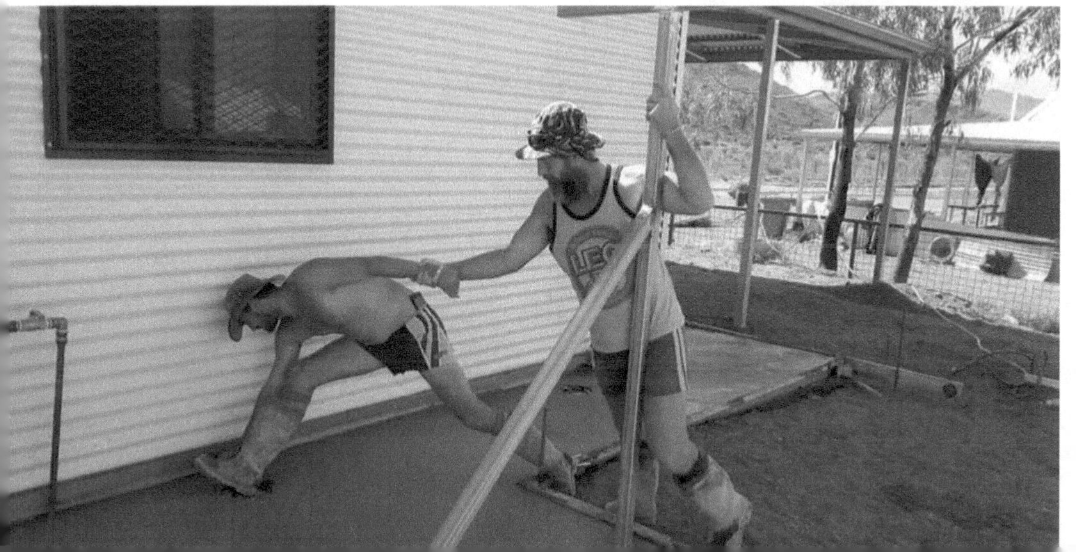

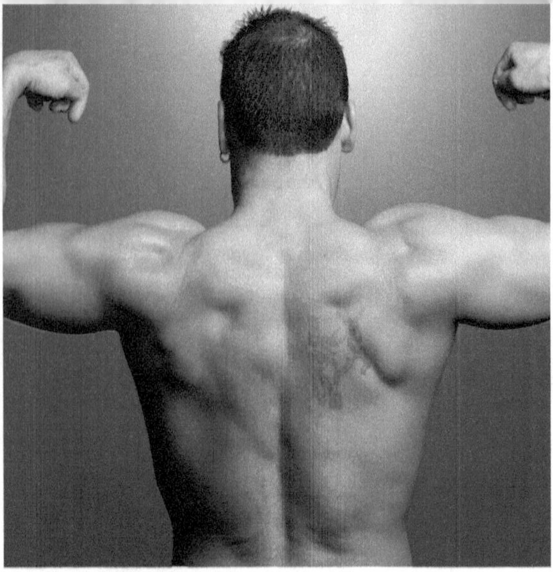
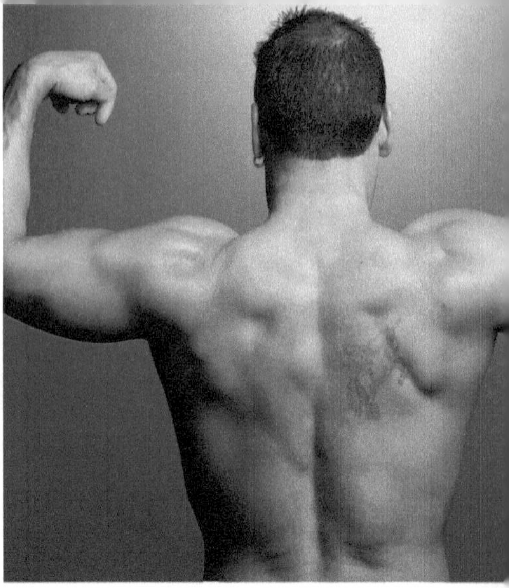
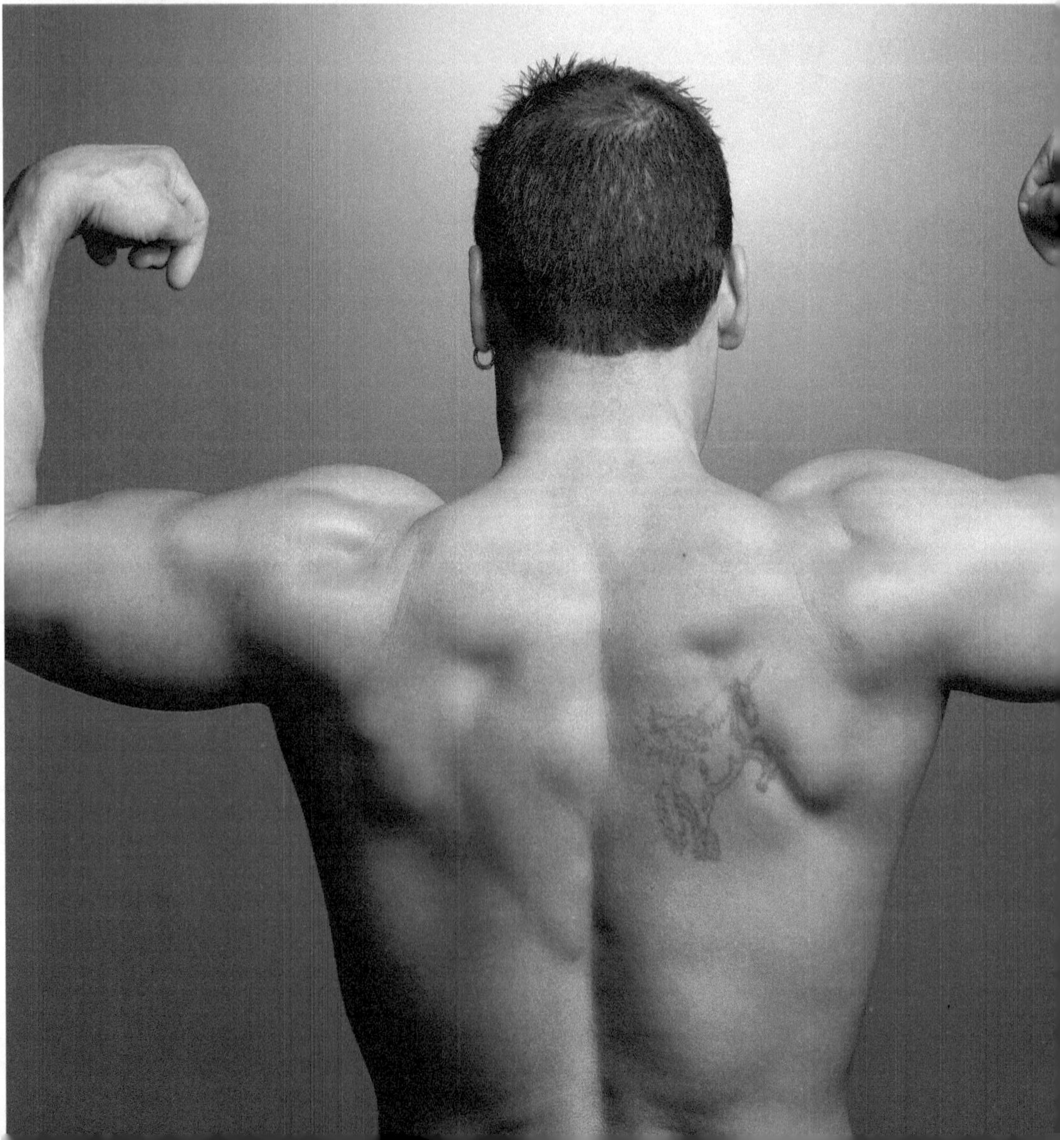

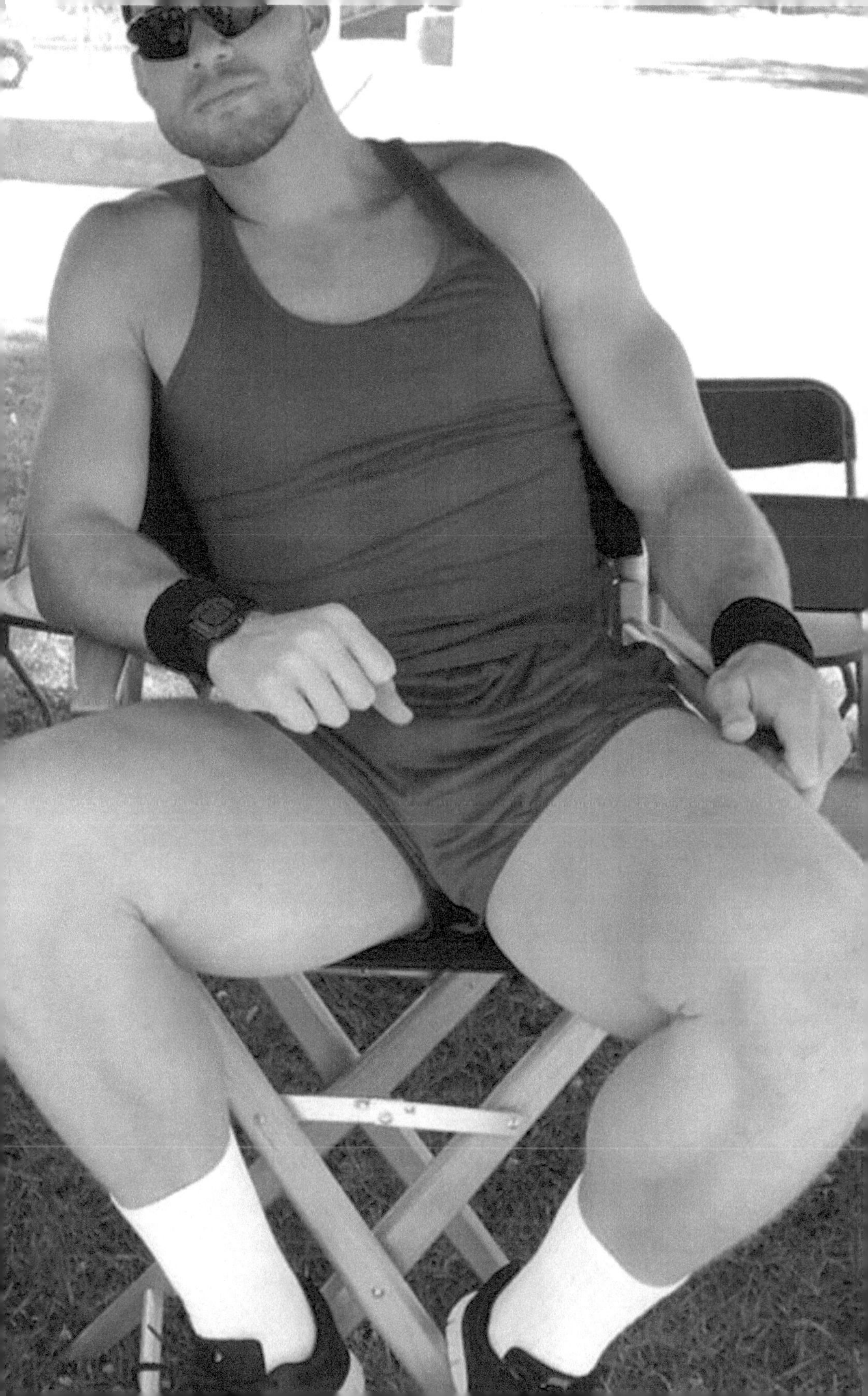

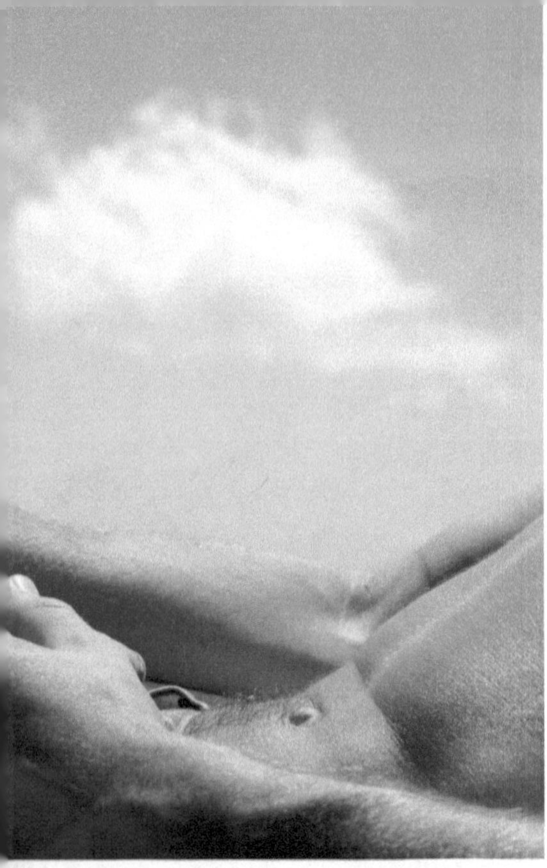
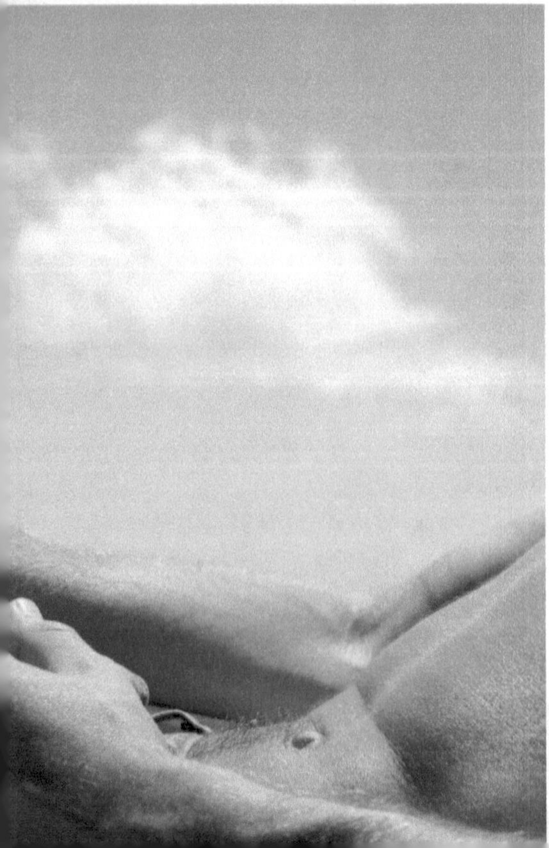

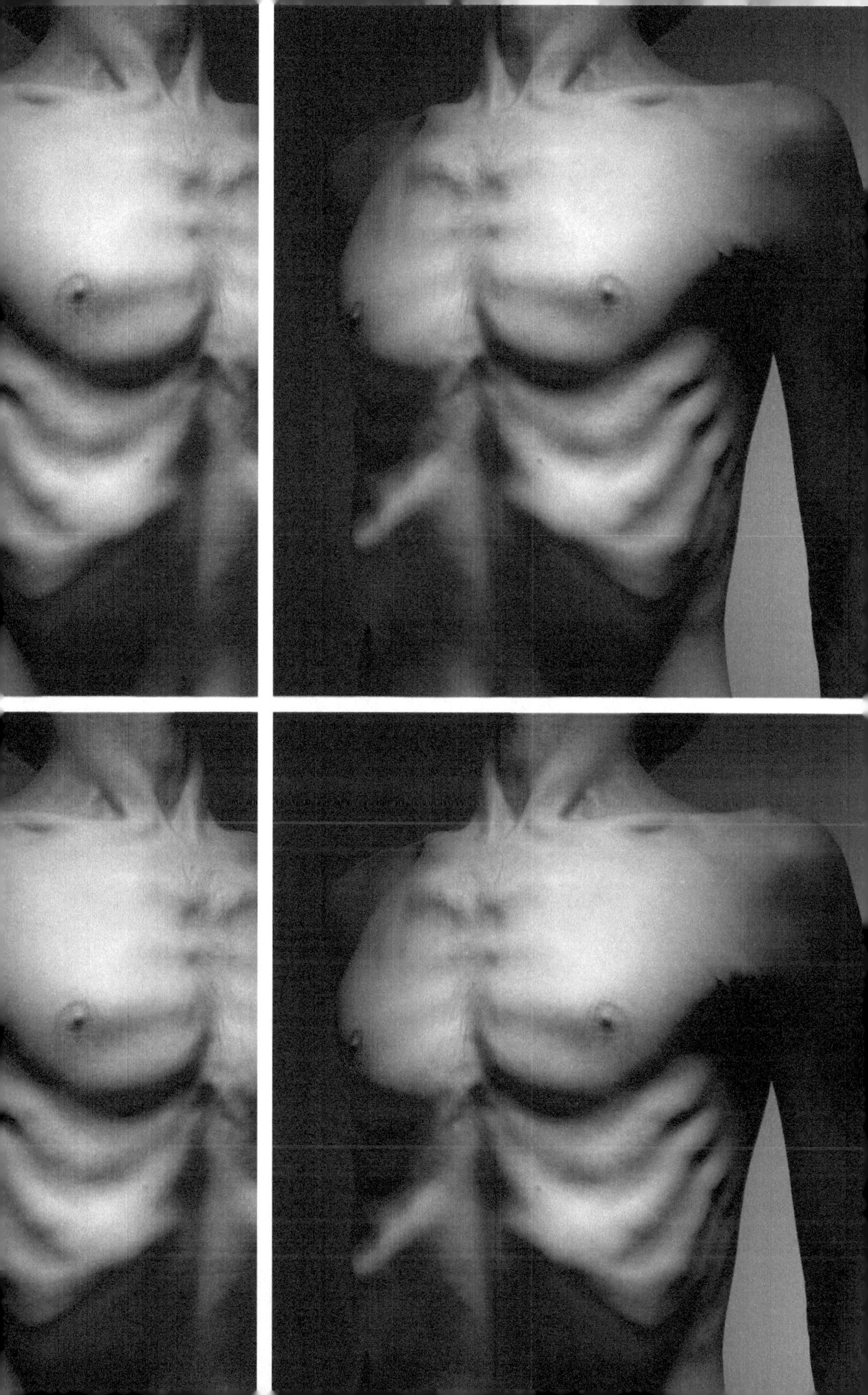

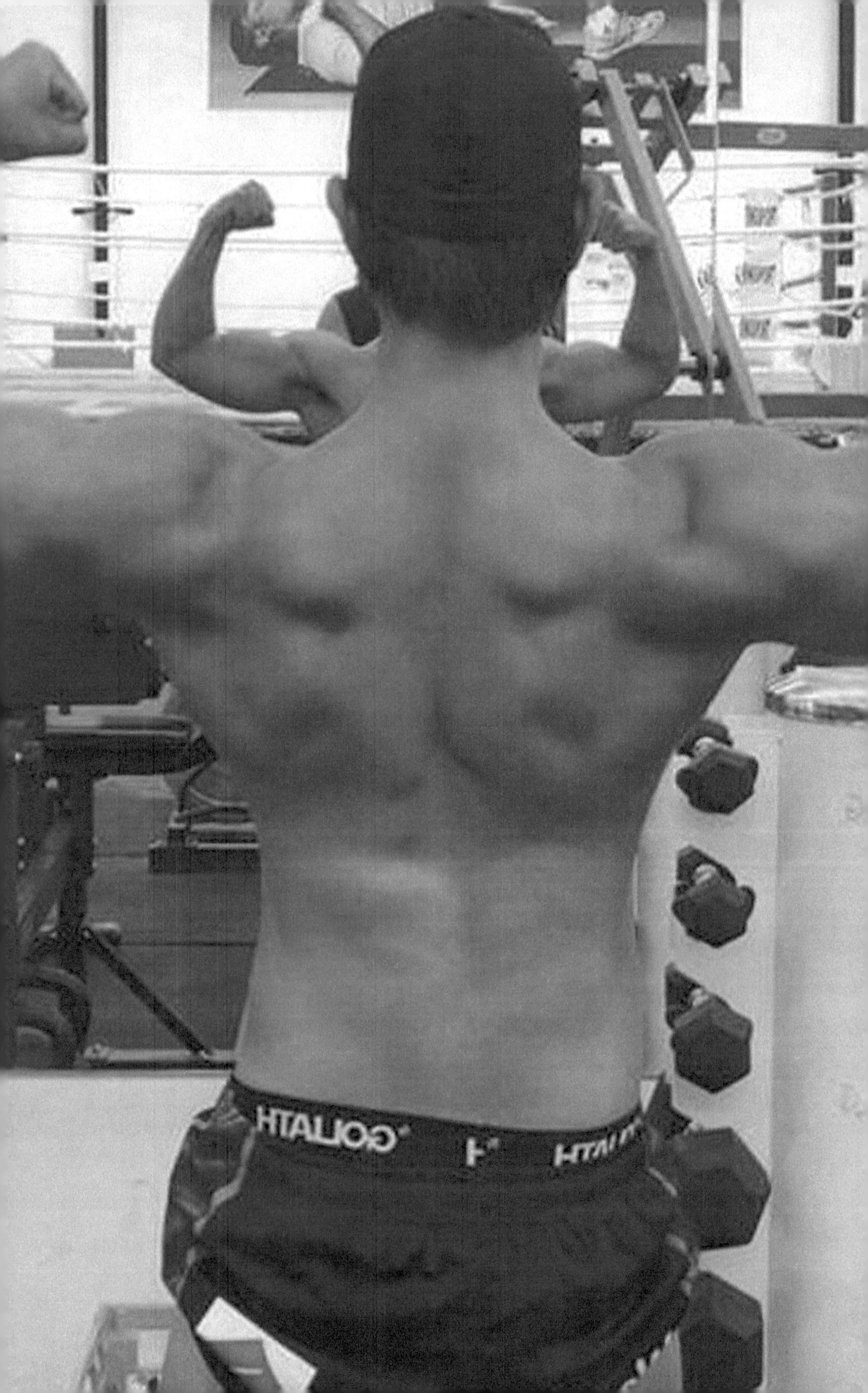

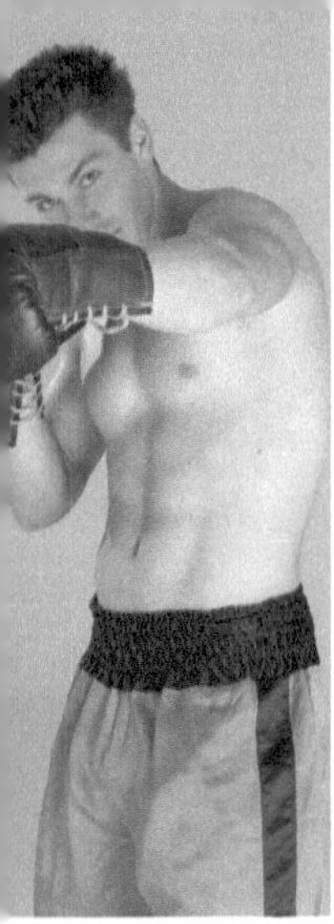
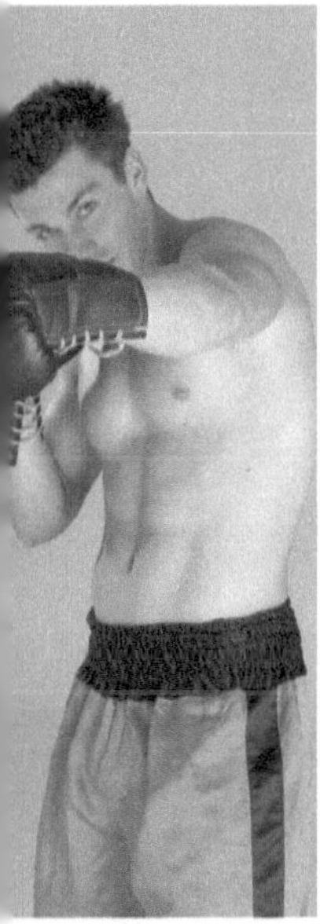
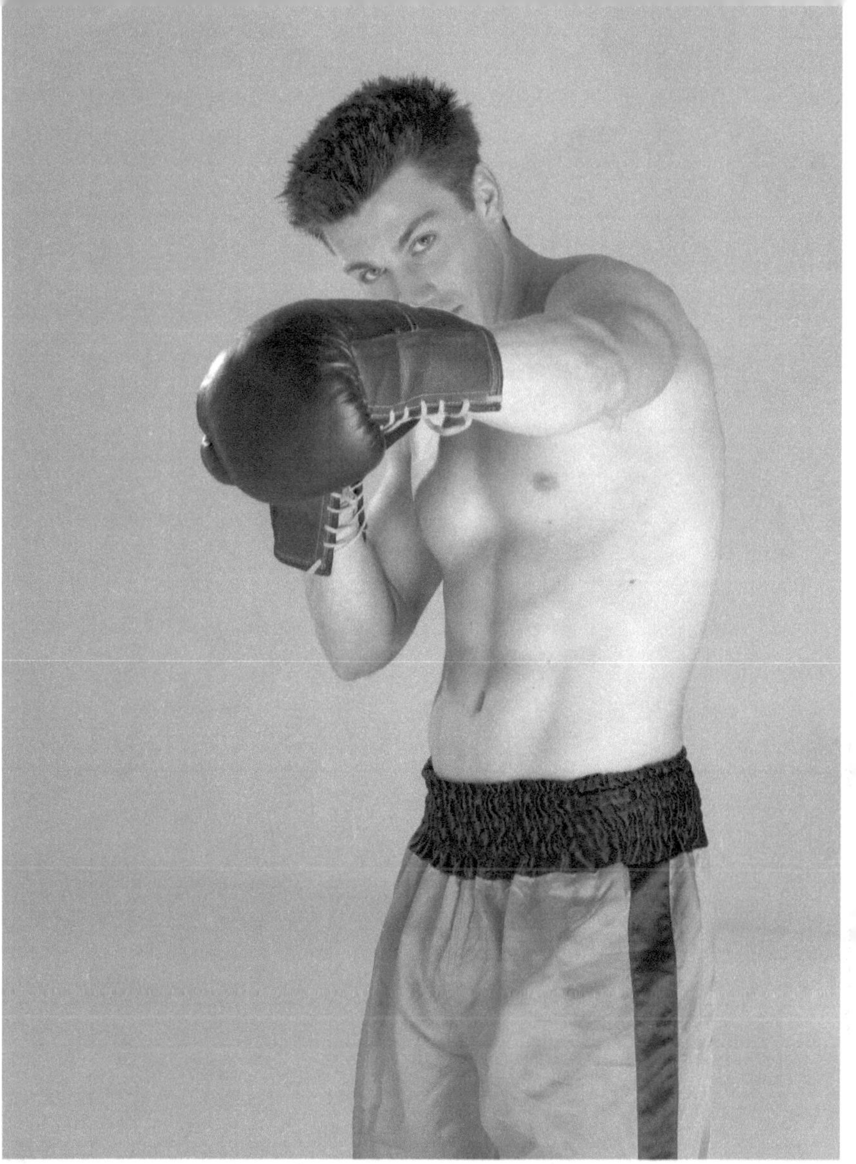
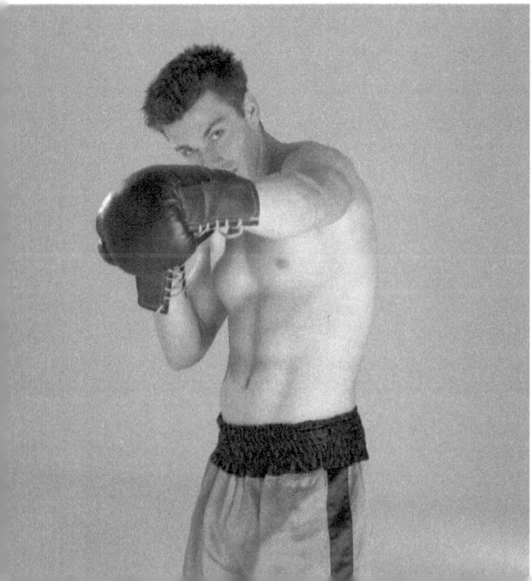
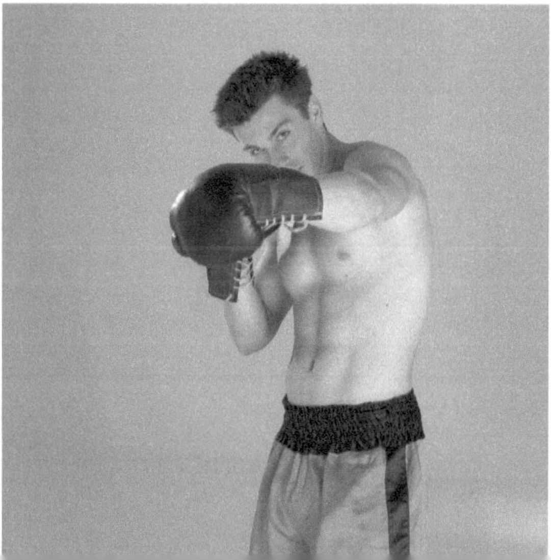

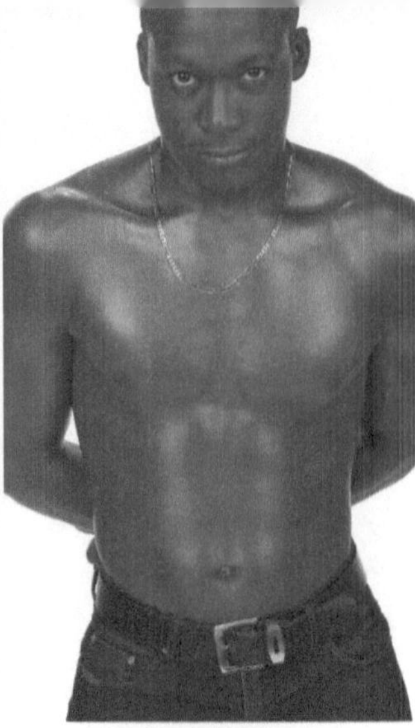
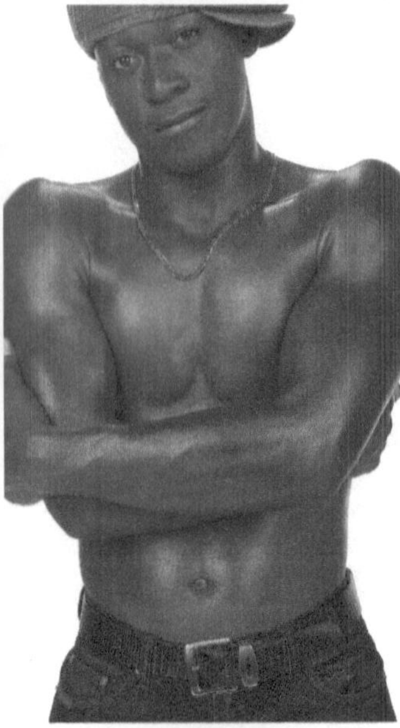
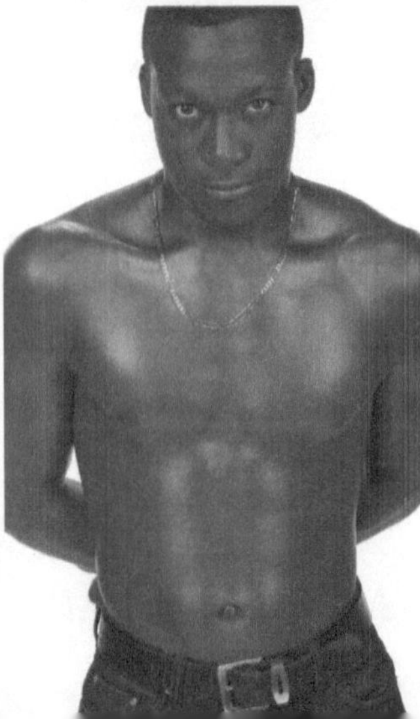
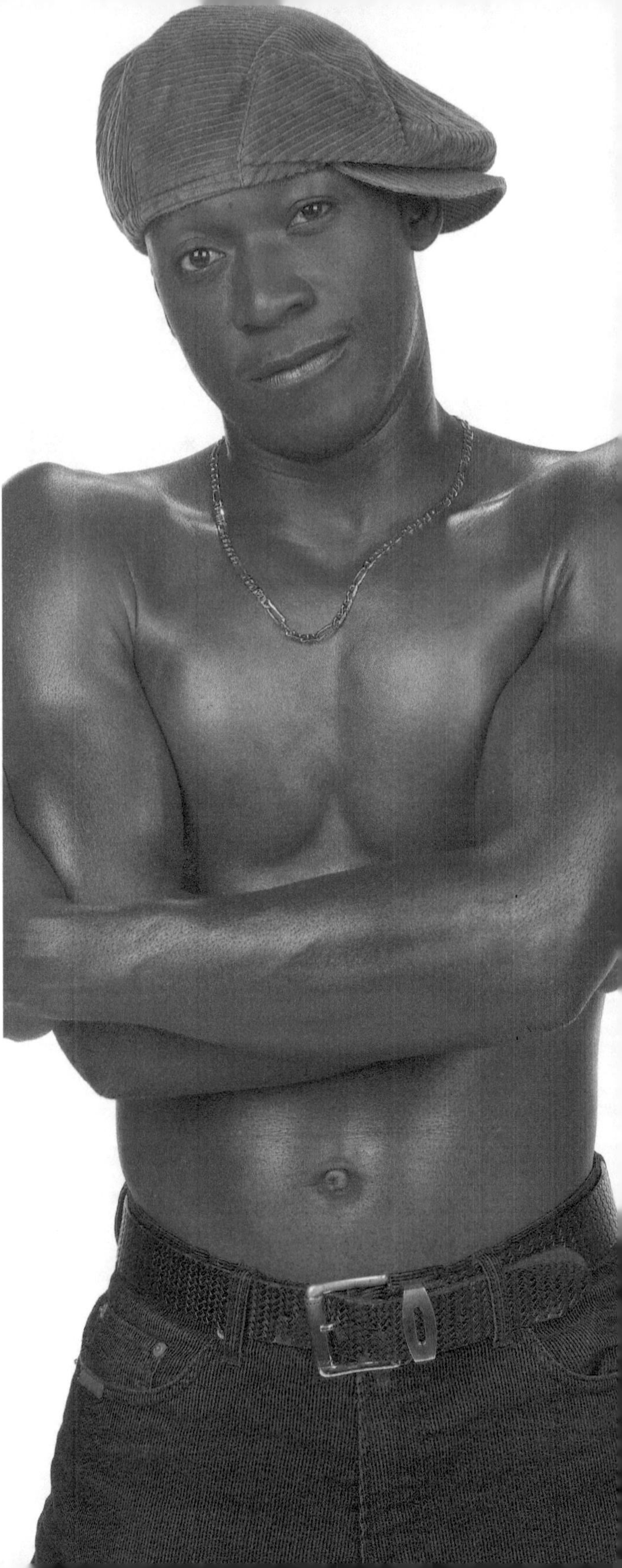

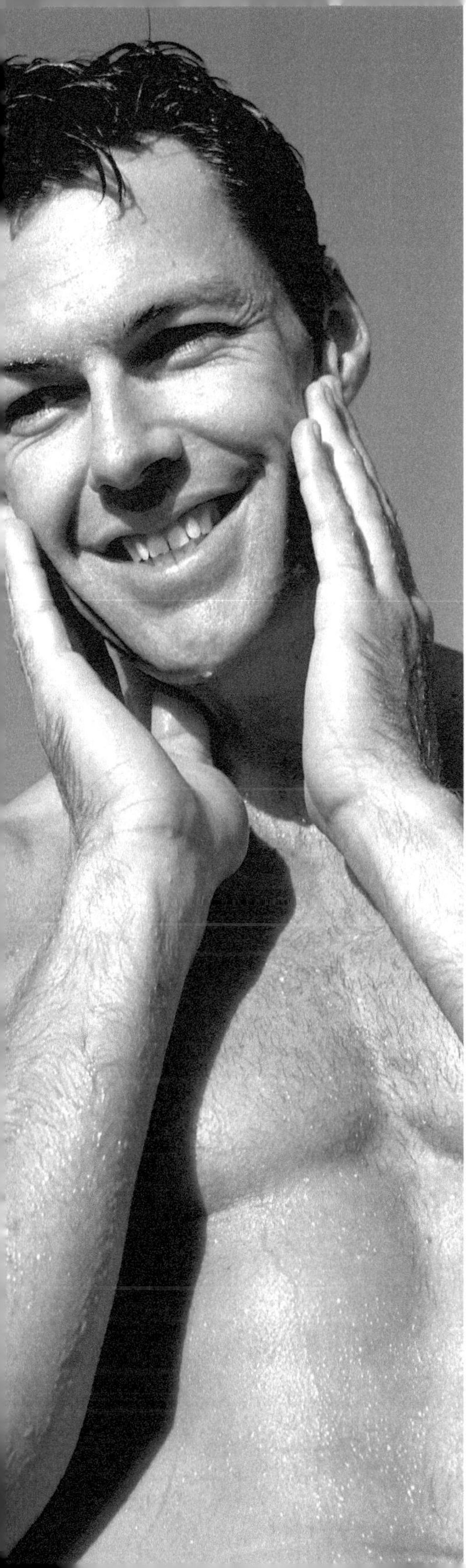
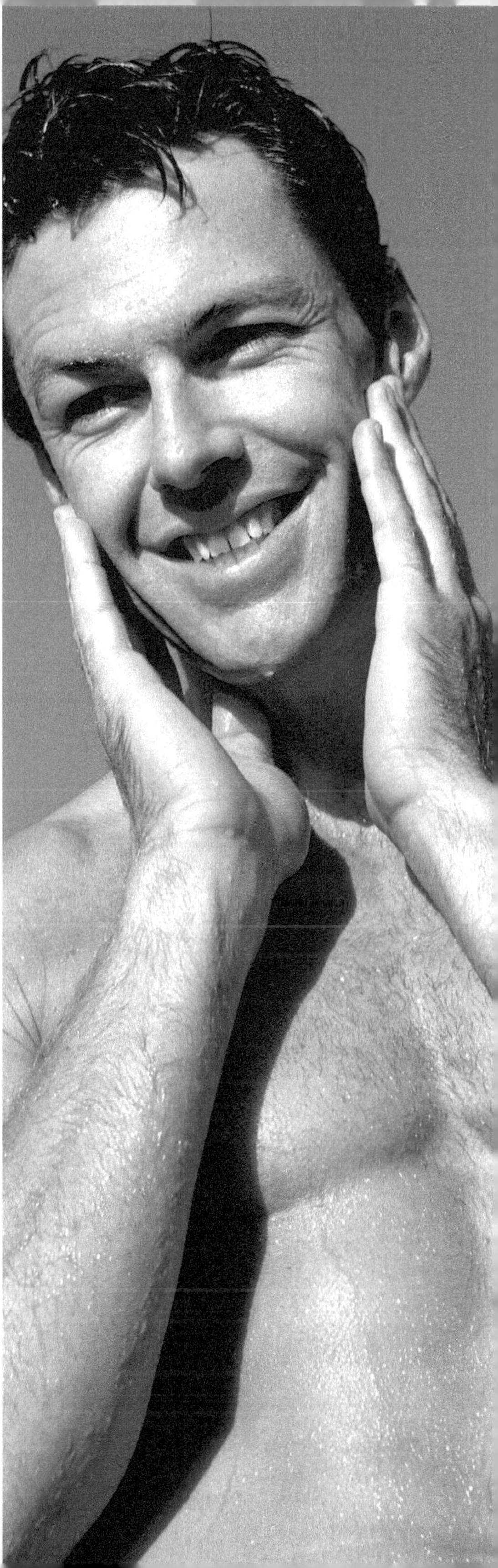

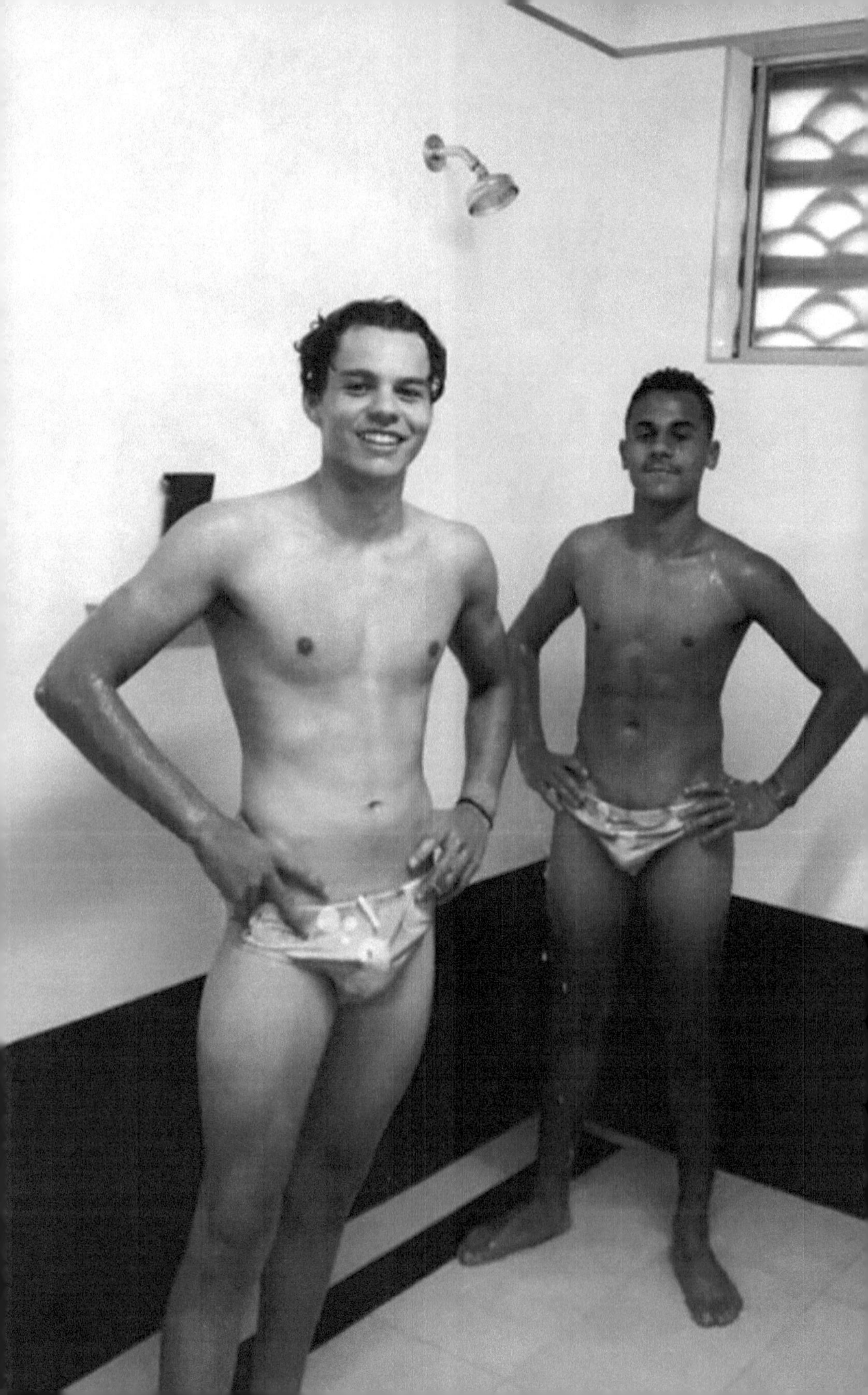

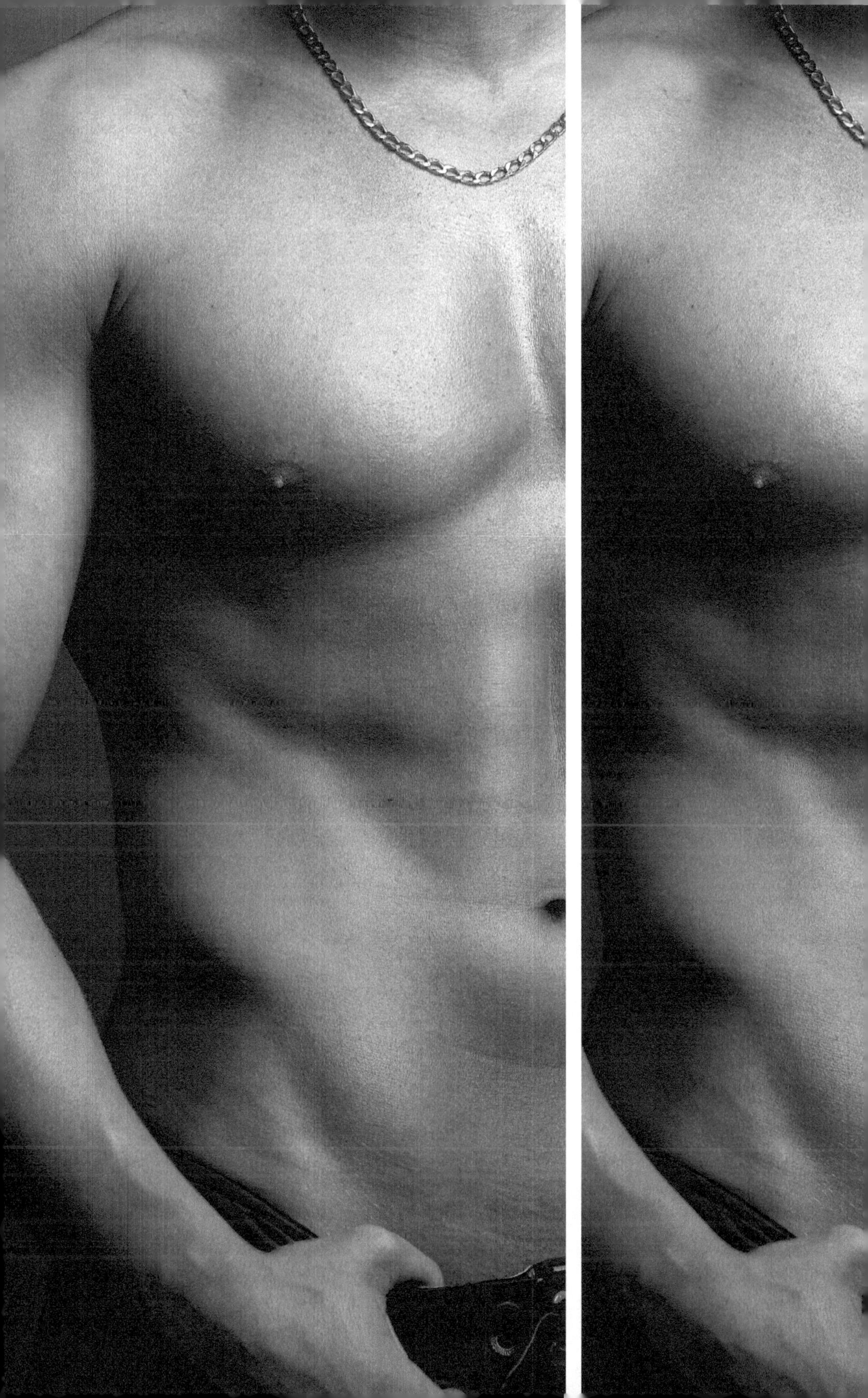

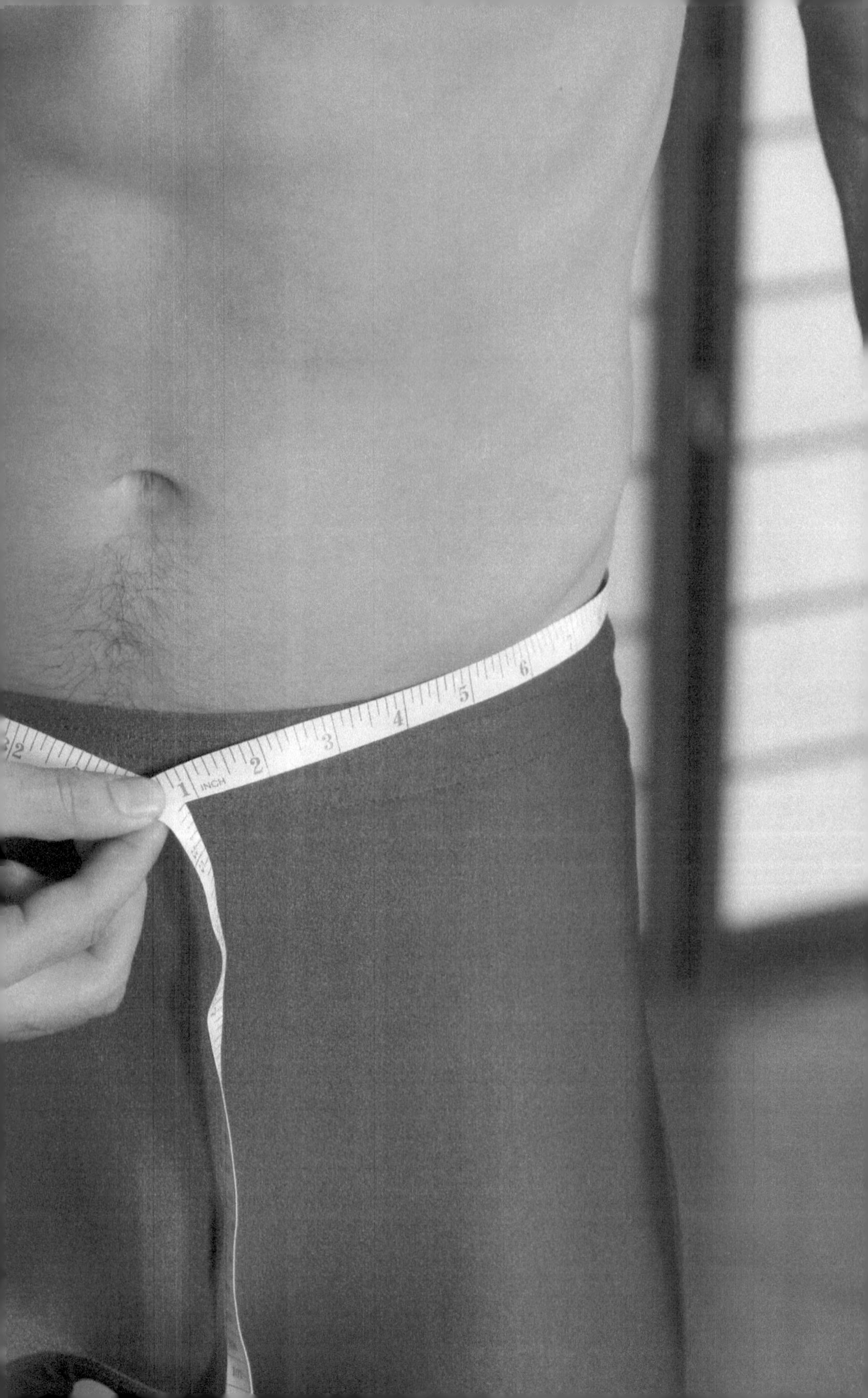
1 INCH 2 3 4 5 6

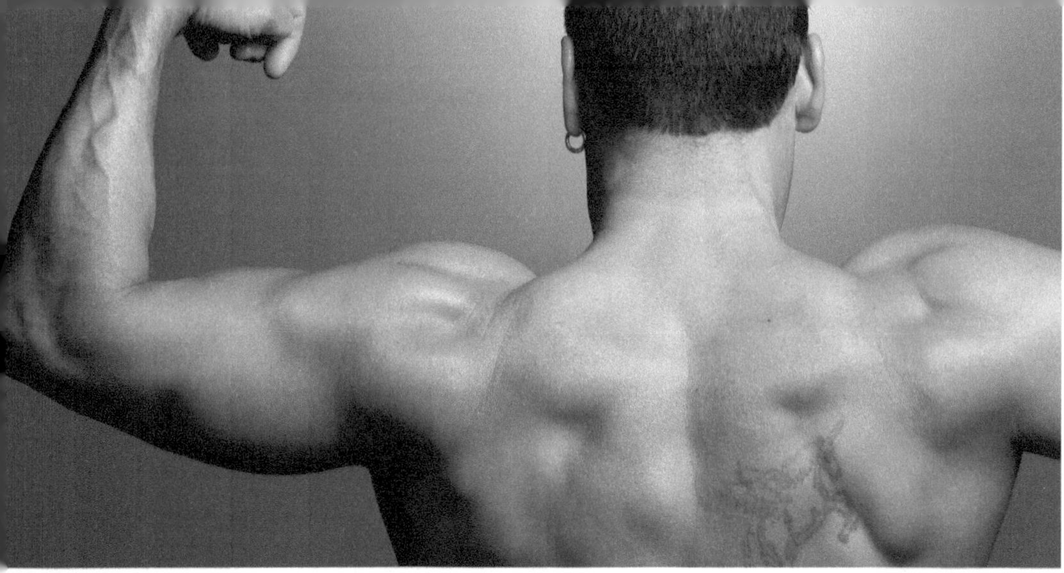
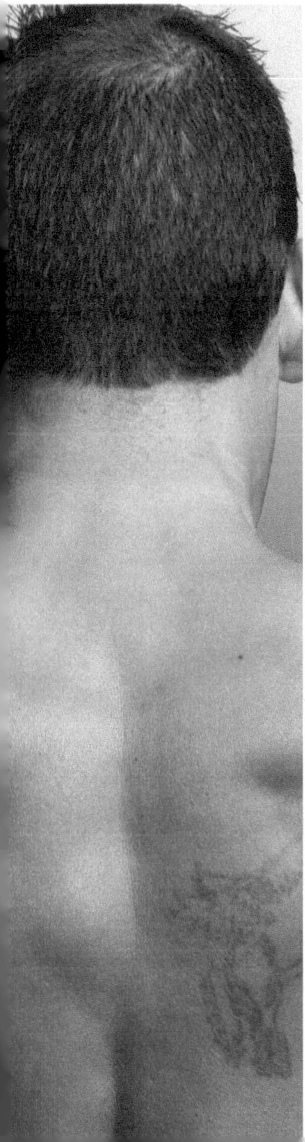
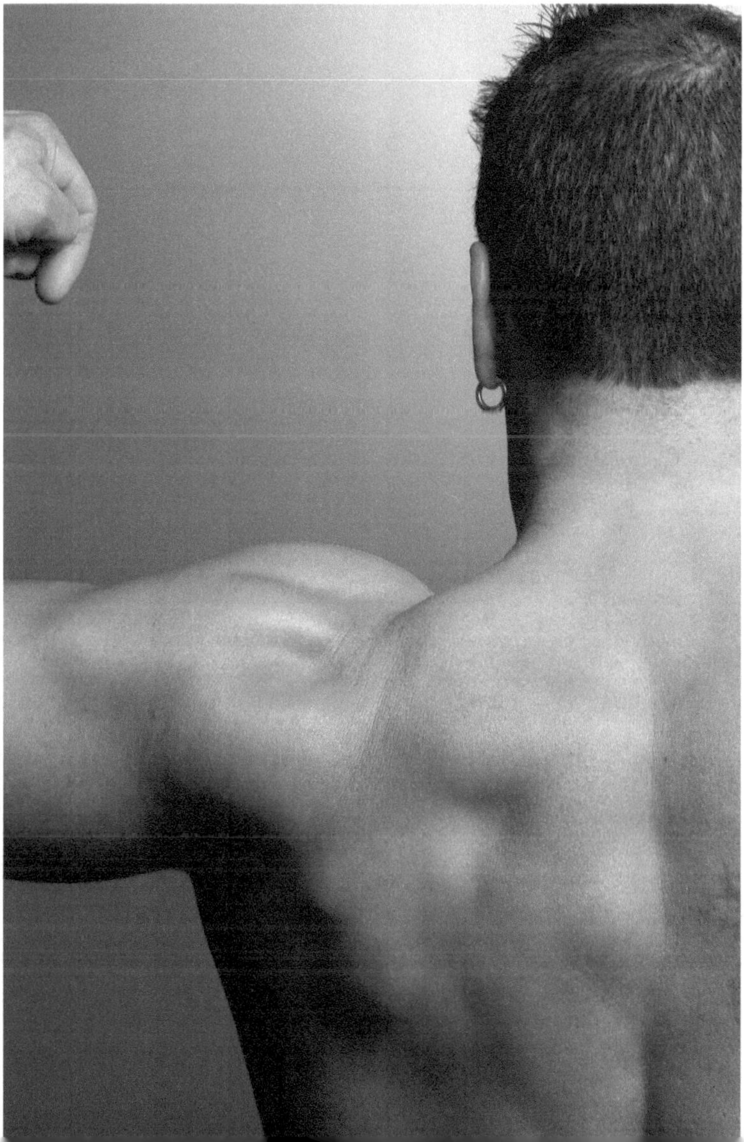

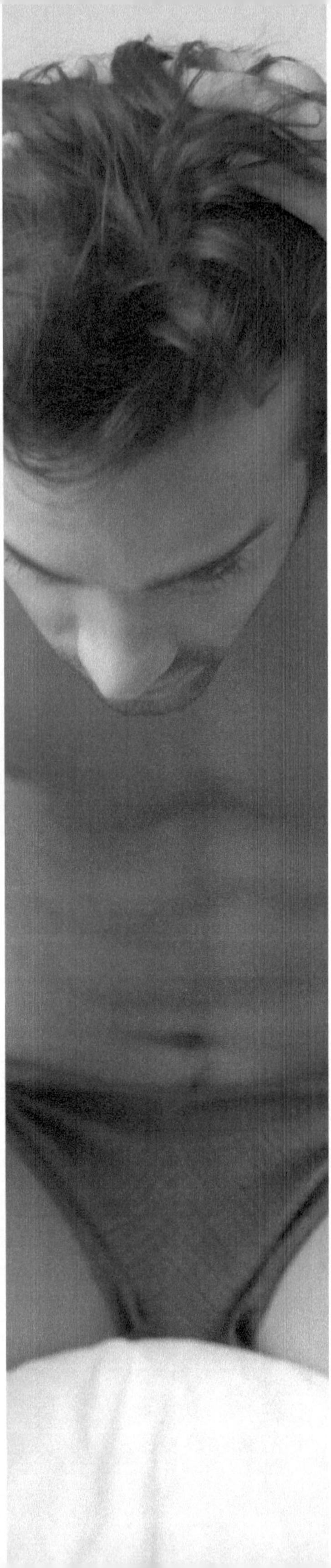
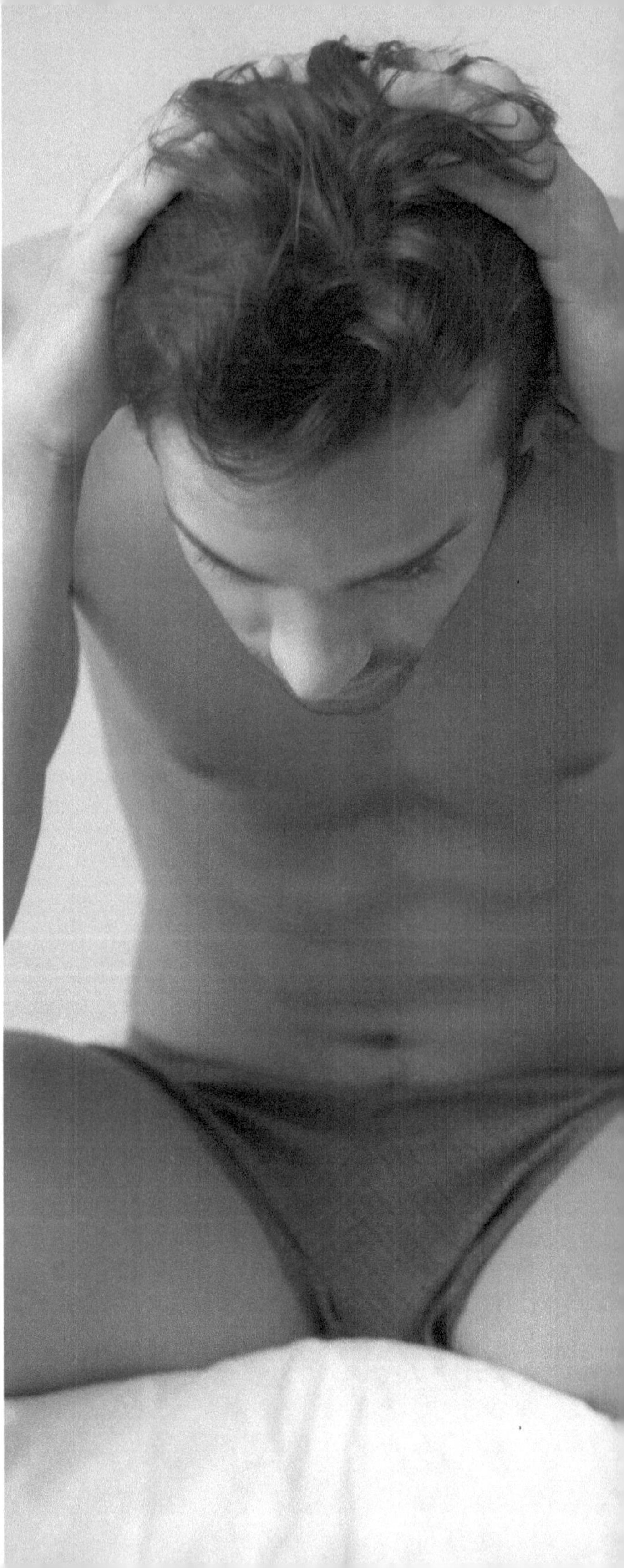

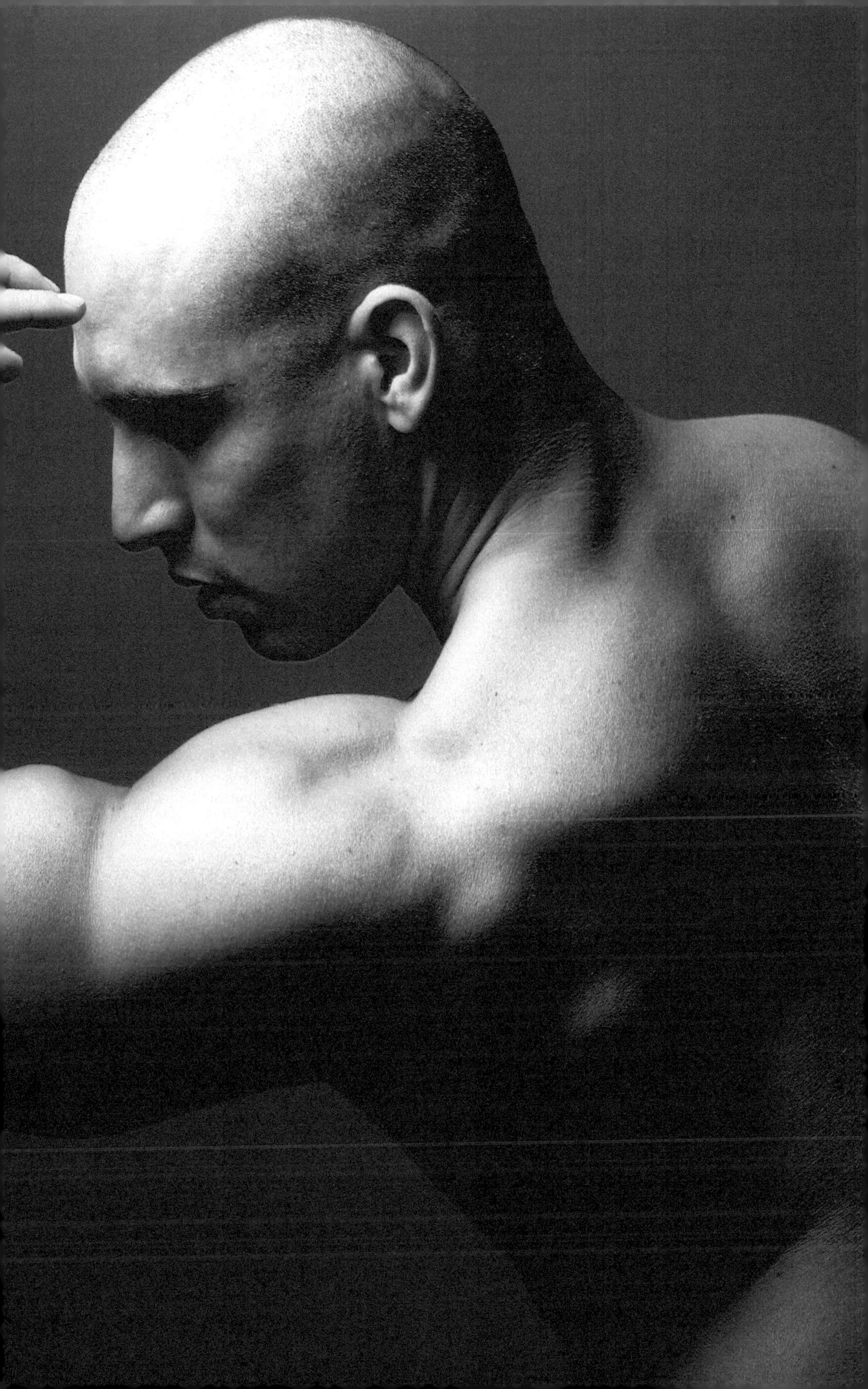

www.ingramcontent.com/pod-product-compliance
Lightning Source LLC
Chambersburg PA
CBHW021023180526
45163CB00005B/2086
9780359965717